Mordecai Richler

Mordecai Richler

by M.G. VASSANJI

With an Introduction by
John Ralston Saul
SERIES EDITOR

EXTRAORDINARY
CANADIANS

PENGUIN CANADA

Published by the Penguin Group

Penguin Group (Canada), 90 Eglinton Avenue East, Suite 700, Toronto,
Ontario, Canada M4P 2Y3 (a division of Pearson Canada Inc.)

Penguin Group (USA) Inc., 375 Hudson Street, New York, New York 10014, U.S.A.
Penguin Books Ltd, 80 Strand, London WC2R 0RL, England
Penguin Ireland, 25 St Stephen's Green, Dublin 2, Ireland
(a division of Penguin Books Ltd)
Penguin Group (Australia), 250 Camberwell Road, Camberwell, Victoria 3124, Australia
(a division of Pearson Australia Group Pty Ltd)
Penguin Books India Pvt Ltd, 11 Community Centre, Panchsheel Park,
New Delhi – 110 017, India
Penguin Group (NZ), 67 Apollo Drive, Rosedale, North Shore 0745, Auckland,
New Zealand (a division of Pearson New Zealand Ltd)
Penguin Books (South Africa) (Pty) Ltd, 24 Sturdee Avenue, Rosebank,
Johannesburg 2196, South Africa

Penguin Books Ltd, Registered Offices: 80 Strand, London WC2R 0RL, England

First published 2009

1 2 3 4 5 6 7 8 9 10 (RRD)

Author representation: Westwood Creative Artists
94 Harbord Street, Toronto, Ontario M5S 1G6

Manufactured in the U.S.A.

LIBRARY AND ARCHIVES CANADA CATALOGUING IN PUBLICATION

Vassanji, M. G
Mordecai Richler / M.G. Vassanji.

(Extraordinary Canadians)
ISBN 978-0-670-06672-8

1. Richler, Mordecai, 1931–2001.   2. Novelists, Canadian (English)—20th
century—Biography.   3. Authors, Canadian (English)—20th
century—Biography.   4. Jewish authors—Canada—Biography.
I. Title.   II. Series: Extraordinary Canadians

PS8535.I38 Z88 2009   C813'.54   C2009-900458-5

Visit the Penguin Group (Canada) website at www.penguin.ca

Special and corporate bulk purchase rates available; please see
www.penguin.ca/corporatesales or call 1-800-810-3104, ext. 477 or 474

This book was printed on 30% PCW recycled paper

For Shahbanu and Edward Goldberg

CONTENTS

Introduction by John Ralston Saul   IX

1   Always the Writer   I

2   Origins   9

3   Out in the World   45

4   An Expatriate in London   71

5   Duddy Kravitz and Away   103

6   The Writer as Family Man   117

7   Goodbye, London; The Embrace of Canada   139

8   The Haunted Jew   157

9   "Maw" and Mutkele   189

10 Engaging with Canada   201

11 True to Himself to the Last   219

SOURCES   227
ACKNOWLEDGMENTS   233
CHRONOLOGY   235

John Ralston Saul

How do civilizations imagine themselves? One way is for each of us to look at ourselves through our society's most remarkable figures. I'm not talking about hero worship or political iconography. That is a danger to be avoided at all costs. And yet people in every country do keep on going back to the most important people in their past.

This series of Extraordinary Canadians brings together rebels, reformers, martyrs, writers, painters, thinkers, political leaders. Why? What is it that makes them relevant to us so long after their deaths?

For one thing, their contributions are there before us, like the building blocks of our society. More important than that are their convictions and drive, their sense of what is right and wrong, their willingness to risk all, whether it be their lives, their reputations, or simply being wrong in public. Their ideas, their triumphs and failures, all of these somehow constitute a mirror of our society. We look at these people, all dead, and discover what we have been, but also what we can be. A mirror is an instrument for measuring ourselves. What we see can be both a warning and an encouragement.

These eighteen biographies of twenty key Canadians are centred on the meaning of each of their lives. Each of them is very different, but these are not randomly chosen great figures. Together they produce a grand sweep of the creation of modern Canada, from our first steps as a democracy in 1848 to our questioning of modernity late in the twentieth century.

All of them except one were highly visible on the cutting edge of their day while still in their twenties, thirties, and forties. They were young, driven, curious. An astonishing level of fresh energy surrounded them and still does. We in the twenty-first century talk endlessly of youth, but power today is often controlled by people who fear the sort of risks and innovations embraced by everyone in this series. A number of them were dead—hanged, infected on a battlefield, broken by their exertions—well before middle age. Others hung on into old age, often profoundly dissatisfied with themselves.

Each one of these people has changed you. In some cases you know this already. In others you will discover how through these portraits. They changed the way the world hears music, thinks of war, communicates. They changed how each of us sees what surrounds us, how minorities are treated, how we think of immigrants, how we look after each other, how we imagine ourselves through what are now our stories.

You will notice that many of them were people of the word. Not just the writers. Why? Because civilizations are built around many themes, but they require a shared public language. So Laurier, Bethune, Douglas, Riel, LaFontaine, McClung, Trudeau, Lévesque, Big Bear, even Carr and Gould, were masters of the power of language. Beaverbrook was one of the most powerful newspaper publishers of his day. Countries need action and laws and courage. But civilization is not a collection of prime ministers. Words, words, words—it is around these that civilizations create and imagine themselves.

The authors I have chosen for each subject are not the obvious experts. They are imaginative, questioning minds from among our leading writers and activists. They have, each one of them, a powerful connection to their subject. And in their own lives, each is engaged in building what Canada is now becoming.

That is why a documentary is being filmed around each subject. Images are yet another way to get at each subject and to understand their effect on us.

The one continuous, essential voice of biography since 1961 has been the *Dictionary of Canadian Biography.* But there has not been a project of book-length biographies such as Extraordinary Canadians in a hundred years, not since the Makers of Canada series. And yet every generation understands the past differently, and so sees in the mirror of these remarkable figures somewhat different lessons. As history rolls on, some truths remain the same while others are revealed in a new and unexpected way.

What strikes me again and again is just how dramatically ethical decisions figured in these people's lives. They form the backbone of history and memory. Some of them, Big Bear, for example, or Dumont, or even Lucy Maud Montgomery, thought of themselves as failures by the end of their lives. But the ethical cord that was strung taut through their work has now carried them on to a new meaning and even greater strength, long after their deaths.

Each of these stories is a revelation of the tough choices unusual people must make to find their way. And each of us as readers will find in the desperation of the Chinese revolution, the search for truth in fiction, the political and military dramas, different meanings that strike a personal chord. At first it is that personal emotive link to such figures which draws us in. Then we find they are a key that opens the whole society of their time to us. Then we realize that in that 150-year period many of them knew each other, were friends, opposed each other. Finally, when all these stories are put together, you will see that a whole new debate has been created around Canadian civilization and the shape of our continuous experiment.

Mordecai Richler cuts across a half-century of Canadian writing and mythmaking in a way that is continually surprising. His ability to find creative truth in the Jewish community of Montreal has become central to the image Canadians as a whole have of themselves at home and abroad. The southern, urban novelist was the one to make the Arctic a reality for everyone, as only a great fiction writer can. By driving his literary knife into every aspect of Canadian self-congratulation, he created our modern standards of creative edge. M.G. Vassanji has an unparalleled skill for making one community's story everyone's story. And so here he has created a literary biography—because Richler was a great writer who lives on through his words—that reflects the imagination of each of us.

CHAPTER ONE

Always the Writer

In 1954 a young writer, having just published his first novel in London, says to a somewhat bemused studio interviewer, "I don't want to be respected, man, I just want to be accepted." There is a certain nerviness to his manner, an edgy defiance in that direct gaze that will become a trademark, on that face that will age and crumple to become, a half-century later, iconic in his home country. At twenty-three it is no small feat he has achieved. He now belongs to the select company of published novelists, among whom he can count the titans who inspired him not so very long ago. The question is what he will make of himself, what kind of writer *he* will become. There is apprehension, to be sure, but the ambition is boundless, the self-confidence supreme. Not long after that interview, he would declare to a friend, "I don't consider myself a Jewish or Canadian writer. I am a writer." Like many another young artist having arrived in the metropolis from a province, he defiantly refuses to be corralled as a provincial or "ethnic," for such a label becomes ultimately a way to belittle, disregard, excuse. He will be judged by his writing; he will not be excused or patronized.

Mordecai Richler had dropped out of college to go to Europe and become a writer, away from what he perceived as a small-minded, limiting Canada and a stifling Montreal Orthodox Jewish community. He could not escape these origins, nor did he deny them. If anything, they came to obsess him. Through most of his adult life, it was these two inheritances—on the one hand, a small nation with only a thin veneer of history, as he saw it, culturally and politically inconsequential on the world stage, and on the other, an ancient tradition with a baggage of too much history and tradition—that he battled to come to terms with.

Nations become small by their genius escaping them; great artists inevitably mature to refashion the cultural map of their day. Fortunately for Canada, Richler's imagination constantly returned to the "ghetto" of his native city, the clamorous, enclosed world of his childhood. It inspired his acclaimed fiction, comical and entertaining and yet bearing the imprint of grim and large collective memories. His novels and his very presence—even at a distance—brought much-needed tonic to an English-Canadian literature long benumbed under the weight of its own inheritance, infusing it with new language, new themes, an often rambunctious irreverence and wit, and lively controversy. He might well be called an early postcolonial novelist, one of those who, coming from a province or colony, extended the scope of the novel in English. Like any expatriate writer, finally, he was faced with a choice: to be influenced by absence or to return home. Richler chose to return to Canada.

What was Canada to him? Jewishness he knew intimately; he was a descendant on his mother's side of a long line of Orthodox rabbis. Montreal, too, he was intimate with, at least the area where he grew up and how it related to the rest of the city. Canada as a nation, however, was more abstract and distant; as a child of Jewish immigrants, he had thought it belonged to "them"—the WASPs. As an adult, therefore, he had to rediscover and claim it, and engage with it even as it reinvented itself with increasing rapidity, and defend it when it threatened to come apart at the seams in which he had been raised, until today he is considered one of its central, and indeed defining, cultural figures of the twentieth century.

He was always highly controversial. His antipathy toward mediocrity and "boosterism," which he satirized with the utmost relish, earned him the ire of cultural nationalists; his fictional portrayals of Jews caused offence in sections of the community. His references to women and race in his novels raised concerns. His send-ups of the more absurd claims of political correctness earned him accusations of picking on easy targets. His observations of his native Quebec raised storms of protest and also shouts of approval. His reply was that he did not write to please. He was a witness to his time. Eventually the charges of self-hate and betrayal which had been hurled at him lost much of their sting, proving that he had been ahead of his time, and he came to be respected for what he was: a gifted novelist and a witty commentator who remained, essentially, honest and called it as he saw it.

I FIRST MET MORDECAI RICHLER at a festival in Sydney, Australia. I had just published my first novel; he was about to win a prize for yet another one. Among the places where we read to audiences was a bookstore, its narrow aisles crammed with people, its acoustics depressing. For me, an unknown in this kind of milieu, the experience was a nightmare. I recall Richler's sympathy and encouragement during that occasion and his telling me I should do more justice to my work in my readings, I had spent time on it, it was mine. He of course was doing fine, riding on fame, fortified by Scotch, his elegant wife, Florence, by his side. I would discover later that he did not like readings either. What impressed me that time, however, was that he had considered me just another Canadian writer, albeit inexperienced, when he could have stuck up his nose and been the haughty celebrity. That was not his style. I met him a few years later at one of those lavish dinner events where writers, much to their embarrassment, find themselves having a good time. We happened to emerge from the stifling hall for air and met in the lobby, where he told me he visited Toronto regularly, we should get together for a chat. I agreed, very flattered; but the opportunity never came; and what would we have spoken about? Neither of us was the chatty type. But at a reading I subsequently gave in London, I discovered that he had asked his daughter to attend. Still a few years later we again met outside the same hall as our previous fruitless tryst and sat down together, away from the din. We nodded to each other and stared silently before us.

When I was asked to write a biography for Penguin about an extraordinary Canadian, I knew of only two such characters who could possibly interest me. One was Mordecai Richler. Here was a chance to get to know him. That I would be able to compensate for the one or possibly more chats we never had seemed a funny twist of fate. We had more in common, I soon realized, than sitting beside each other staring silently ahead, unable to start a conversation. We both grew up in an urban colonial setting, in closed, religiously observant, jealous communities. One in Montreal, the other in Dar es Salaam, Tanzania. Who could have guessed such a commonality in two such diverse lives? If I may indulge in a curious coincidence, it is this: the first place I stayed when I arrived in Canada from the United States was on Jeanne Mance Street in Montreal, where Richler's fearsome grandfather Shmariyahu had lived, and where Richler recalled being belted by the old man for religious non-observance. I had not heard of Mordecai Richler then.

MORDECAI RICHLER left prodigious information about himself. His archives are vast. His novels freely and profusely use material from his life, and he has also written directly about his childhood and literary apprenticeship. He constantly wrote and received letters, the more so during his two decades away from Canada. Besides his novels and stories, he published two works of non-fiction, a clutch of television and film scripts, and a large number of columns and essays. He is a Canadian legend about whom numerous anecdotes are told. Paradoxically, he was also a very private man, a trickster character who did not readily reveal himself. He did not confide in journals; his letters speak of his writing life, his plans, ephemera about his current life and work and sometimes the family. His inner worries and anxieties, the aching wounds and scars of an intense, driven man of "appetite" who is a writer, are not exposed for all to see. When he does occasionally reveal that tender core, we are shocked.

My purpose in this book has been to describe the man Mordecai Richler, as I have come to discover him, based on what I hope has been a judicious and consistent selection of material. Anecdotes I have listened to with amusement, for they are amusing, but not relied on in my construction. Memories of him, of which numerous exist, I have treated with caution; what people recall of a person or an event most often are only isolated moments, and as such tend to be the odd or the uncharacteristic or rare occasion, the offhand remark; moreover, who, getting on in age, doesn't use memory to embellish, reinvent, settle scores? This becomes glaringly evident when we come across memories that actually conflict with one another.

I have attempted to distance my character from the gruff caricature, the "classic Richler" that the media loved. He undoubtedly entertained and made news with that demeanour, using it to provoke controversy, to call on the detractors and the cheerleaders. But that was only one, and a later, aspect of him—playing on a celebrity status, the hazards of which he had sternly warned against as a younger, hungrier man. Mordecai Richler was first a literary man, a disciplined, professional writer and novelist of great distinction. A complex man of many qualities who carried on not just the much-reported public battles but also his private inner struggles. He was not always consistent—who is, at any one time, let alone during a lifetime? He was ambitious as a young man but circumscribed by his origins, with which, however, he made his peace; a controversial truth-teller ready to demolish an extreme or ludicrous position, yet not always quite sensitive to the truth lurking behind it; a devoted family man; and a generous dearly loved friend. A man who escaped, discovered himself, and returned, but stayed at an angle with his world, always the exile, the writer.

CHAPTER TWO

Origins

Mordecai Richler was born on January 27, 1931, into an Orthodox Jewish family in Montreal, in the downtown neighbourhood that he called, despite objections, the ghetto, a thin urban grid consisting of the five working-class streets between St. Laurent Boulevard (the Main) and Park Avenue, bounded below by Pine Avenue and above by St. Viateur. Both sets of grandparents had emigrated from Eastern Europe in the early twentieth century, within living memory. His mother's father, Jehudah Rosenberg, was an eminent Hasidic rabbi and scholar from Poland who had immigrated to Toronto in 1912 before ending up with his large family in Montreal, in 1919, not far away from the Richlers. Mordecai's paternal grandfather, Shmariyahu (Shmarya) Richler, had arrived in 1904 from Galicia, a province of Eastern Europe, and was in the scrap metal business. According to a family story, Shmarya had arrived with an onward fare from Montreal to New York (an alternative story says Chicago), but he met a fellow Galician with a ticket only up to Montreal, where he had no relatives. So the two men exchanged tickets and cities.

The Jews of North America with origins in the same region of Eastern Europe were intimately related in their history and culture, a connection carried over into an easy identification across the Canadian-American border. Many of them had relations on the other side. It would take a generation at least before the essential differences in the two countries would come to be felt in these communities, and accepted.

Naturally the traditions that had been nurtured in the Old World for centuries would reflect on the lives of the Jews of Montreal's Main, and naturally they would come under threat in the generational conflicts that were a part of Richler's growing up. On one side existed the great tradition going back thousands of years, the elaborate rules and rituals, the memories of exile, oppression, and survival; on the other, the exhilarating freedom of North America, the seductions of assimilation, the promise of a new identity in a land of unlimited expanse and opportunity. But even this new promised land was not immune to the bane of anti-Semitism, bringing back to the quick memories of past victimhood. The Holocaust in Europe in the twentieth century only kept those fears alive, the old identity potent.

Jews had lived in Eastern Europe since medieval times and perhaps before, in self-contained villages or urban neighbourhoods called shtetls, in Russia, Poland, Galicia, and elsewhere. Galicia, a province of the Austro-Hungarian Empire, bordered Russia and Poland in the north and occupied a territory now divided between Poland and Ukraine. Unlike their western Sephardic brethren, these Eastern Ashkenazim lived a separate existence from their neighbours, in their case the Poles, Ukrainians, Russians, and Germans. Under the eyes of watchful governments, they essentially governed themselves, with their own rabbinical courts, educational institutions, and voluntary and charitable organizations; they had their butchers, bakers, barbers, circumcisers, teachers, musicians, printers, and middlemen; they had their lawyers, doctors, innkeepers, traders, and wealthy businessmen.

Their language was Yiddish, an inter-territorial hybrid of mainly High German and Hebrew, with small admixtures of other European languages. Their life in the shtetl was defined in finest detail by religion, ritual, and tradition. All acts of daily living, from the morning prayer at waking to washing, eating, and clothing, were to be performed according to prescribed rules and rituals; Sabbath was strictly observed. The traditional male attire was a white shirt, a vest, black pants, a long black caftan, and a black hat. The women dressed modestly and wore wigs. Only a minority of Jews today observe these codes. The life of the Jews in the shtetls is vividly described in the novels of Isaac Bashevis Singer, who was born in Poland in 1902.

Alternately tolerated and despised, the outcasts of mainstream society, victimized, economically restricted, and physically bullied, the Jews did not have a status as a nation as other peoples did. Often, on an authoritarian whim, the shtetls were subjected to organized mass attacks, called pogroms (from the word for "riot" in Russian), and expulsions. Perhaps the most serious attacks on the Jews of Eastern Europe occurred in 1648 under the Ukrainian Chmielnicki, who led a large uprising of Cossacks in the destruction of numerous shtetls and the deaths of many thousands. More recently, in 1903, there was an extremely violent pogrom in Kishinev, Russia, and, in 1918, in Cracow, Poland. Moreover, whenever a bunch of drunks needed a scapegoat, there was always the Jew at hand.

In the eighteenth century, a mystical mass movement called Hasidism took hold among the Jews of Eastern Europe. Founded by Israel ben Eliezer, or the Baal Shem Tov, Hasidism was based on ecstatic devotion to God, in contrast to the formal rabbinical form of the faith, or "rabbinism." Hasidic practice, which involved the person emotionally and completely, was attractive to a simple, vulnerable, and superstitious population devastated by the Cossack uprising of fifty years before and fearful of the ongoing political upheavals of the region. It is estimated that almost half of Eastern European Jewry followed the Hasidic movement. Almost every shtetl had a Hasidic leader, the Rebbe, or Tzaddik, who himself was a subject of devotion and often claimed magical powers. Stories of these miracles became part of the Hasidic traditions.

Since the nineteenth century, Jewish immigration to North America had been progressively on the rise. Leaving a land which had been home for centuries, where they had developed distinct traditions and yet were always the outsiders, was a one-way voyage from an experience of persecution and life on the edge. They came away to Montreal, Chicago, New York, bearing their culture and history and language, their memories of exile and persecution; the conflicts with the new generations, obviously less attached to the old ways, were therefore painful. They are reflected in Mordecai Richler's adolescent rebellion while growing up in Montreal.

THE MONTREAL OF RICHLER'S CHILDHOOD and youth was Canada's cosmopolis and largest port. Situated at the mouth of the St. Lawrence River, it had been since fur-trading days the economic nerve centre of the country and its doorway to the world. A diversity of people therefore came to settle here. Immigrants, even if headed elsewhere, landed at Montreal before going on by train to Toronto, Chicago, New York, or Winnipeg. With its diversity of coexisting peoples and two predominant language cultures, it had a unique character on the North American continent. One aspect of the city's culture was defined by the presence of a wealthy Anglo-Scottish business elite—at the turn of the twentieth century they controlled three-quarters of the wealth of the nation. Enthusiasts of the British Crown, they inhabited the more palatial residences of the city, initially in the area known as the Golden Square Mile and later in Westmount. Among them were the Killams, the Holts, the McConnells, the Molsons, the Southams—industrialists, financiers, newspaper barons—well-known Canadian names to this day. The lesser folk, besides those of British and French descent, included the growing numbers of Jews, Greeks, and Italians.

"Babylon on the St. Lawrence," Montreal, was the city of culture and corruption, nightclubs and churches, of legends and legendary larger-than-life personalities. Prostitution thrived, the police were happily corrupt. "Vice stalks through our city," scolded Judge Coderre in a report in the 1920s, "with a hideousness and insolence that appear sure of immunity." Whorehouse madams flaunted their wealth, he fumed, riding in luxurious automobiles and living in grand mansions in the better sections of the city. Two decades later nothing had changed, according to William Weintraub, Montreal writer and historian. The politics of the city (and province) were no less outrageous, exemplified by its colourful, populist mayor, Camillien Houde, who had emerged from the poverty that was the other face of Montreal.

In 1939, on the eve of the Second World War, Montrealers gave a tumultuous welcome to King George VI and Queen Elizabeth, who were driven in a motorcade around a festooned city packed with flag-waving crowds. Schools were off that day, and among those who waved at the King and Queen from the street was a young Mordecai Richler. The war that came soon highlighted the deep divisions within Quebec society. In 1940 Mayor Houde was held in detention for publicly declaring—and reflecting the French-nationalist sentiment—that he would refuse to register for war service, a requirement for male adults that was to be put into effect shortly. Welcomed by a crowd of thousands when released four years later, he went on to win the mayoral election once again. Meanwhile, during the war the city had seen an eruption of overt anti-Semitism in the form of nasty media pronouncements and painted slogans in public places. Public morality continued to be defended by the Church, and a mass wedding of more than a hundred Catholic couples took place in the baseball stadium, witnessed by more than two thousand well-wishers. This was the larger political and social reality within which the Jews lived in the ghetto, as a mostly self-contained community.

A few months before Houde's release, the lovely stripper Lili St. Cyr began her stint at the Gayety Theatre on the Main, to last seven years, thrilling males from adolescent to senior, one of whom was Mordecai Richler's father, Moses. With her classy-sounding French name, "Montreal's most famous woman" and "Goddess of Love" was actually Marie Klarquist of Minneapolis. "I broke hearts and emptied pocketbooks," she said, while Father Anjou denounced her in *Le Devoir:* "The theatre is made to stink with the foul odour of sexual frenzy." No other city in Canada, perhaps in all North America, could boast such a boisterous cultural mélange, match such excess and repression, reproduce such popular excitement. It was a writer's, or an artist's, dream city, and indeed it was called, with typically colonial hyperbole, the

Paris of the West (or North); but it did produce a host of renowned writers, filmmakers, and playwrights.

Saul Bellow was born in Lachine, a suburb of Montreal, in 1915; the family may have lived in the Jewish ghetto before moving on to Chicago when he was nine. More essentially Canadian but of the same generation and background as Bellow were Irving Layton, born in Romania and brought to Montreal at the age of one in 1913; A.M. Klein, born in Ukraine in 1909 and also perhaps brought to Montreal at age one; and Louis Dudek, born in Montreal in 1918. One cannot help observing that these writers must all have borne the mark of the outrages in Eastern Europe. The latter three went on to become leading Canadian anglophone poets. They attended the same high school (Baron Byng) in the ghetto, on St. Urbain Street, both the school and the street immortalized in the future novels of Mordecai Richler. The city could claim, in addition, poet F.R. Scott, novelist Hugh MacLennan, and humorist Stephen Leacock among its eminent literati and teachers at McGill, which itself was the alma mater of critic and biographer Leon Edel. A younger generation of Montrealers included Mavis Gallant and Leonard Cohen; Brian Moore, an immigrant from Ireland; and William Weintraub, a filmmaker and writer whose lasting contribution may be his accounts of his friendships and his carefully documented correspondence with Richler, Gallant, and Moore during the formative years of their distinguished literary careers.

A TEN-YEAR-OLD with wide dark eyes and protruding ears, a thick mop of black hair, and a somewhat melancholy, mysterious look that would not change even in middle age. He did not deign to smile for the camera. An intense young man hurrying about with a pile of books in his arms. By all accounts he was reserved, sometimes awkward, though as the renowned writer he would become he would captivate admiring audiences even when he did not enjoy addressing them. Mordecai Richler's was not a happy childhood at home, for his parents did not get along and eventually separated. But it was a childhood otherwise rich in character and experience, crowded and eventful, leaving indelible impressions that he would describe in autobiographical essays, capture in his short fiction—collected in *The Street*—and transform into the material of his longer and mature work. This childhood world became his literary universe; it would bring him his glory.

Jews formed the largest immigrant group in Montreal. By 1941, when Richler was ten, there were sixty-four thousand Jews in the city. Arriving at the riverfront quays, the immigrants would have been met by the expansive St. Laurent Boulevard (the Main), which funnelled them up to their respective neighbourhoods. A vast majority settled in the ghetto. In its exclusivity, its closeness to the Orthodox tradition, and its self-sufficiency, this ghetto was simply a more open version of the Eastern European shtetl. Everyone could speak Yiddish, and some spoke nothing but. The Main was where its public life took place, where you would saunter off to buy your meat or bread, or follow the smells to the bagel ovens or to your favourite among half a dozen delis for your smoked meat, or go get your groceries, or have a suit made, or hang around and shoot pool, have a drink and a banter, talk politics, or catch a movie at the Roxy or the Crystal Palace. If you were old enough, you could sneak off to catch Lili St. Cyr perform at the Gayety, if she was in town.

St. Urbain Street was the second street westward from the Main and, in the young Richler's universe, the second step up the ladder of relative prosperity. The bottom rung was Clark Street. Park Avenue was at the top and the dividing line, beyond which was the area of Outremont and its dream life, where the wealthy Jews lived. The boy from the ghetto makes it abundantly clear how far away that life was, how enticing, how impossible it seemed to the poorer Jews like his father. On St. Urbain Street, the men worked as cutters or pressers or scrap dealers and drifted into cold-water flats, sitting down to supper in their freckled Penman's long winter underwear, clipping their nails at the table.

Others worked as shoemakers, deliverymen, mechanics. The cold-water flats in which they lived, in the typical brick row houses of the neighbourhood, were heated only by a single coal stove in the kitchen, leaving the rest of the apartments cold during the harsh winters. In Outremont, beyond Park Avenue, however, the fathers,

in their three-piece suits and natty fedoras, were in property or sweaters or insurance or (the coming thing) plastics. They were learning how to golf.

Outremont, our heart's desire, was amazing. Kids our own age there didn't hang out at the corner cigar store or poolroom, they had their very own quarters. *Basement playrooms, Ping-Pong tables.* There were heated towel racks in the bathrooms. In each kitchen, a Mixmaster.

The Montreal society of those times has been depicted as consisting of three distinct parts—"solitudes," to use a favourite Canadian word—with hardly any social interaction among them, but with enough suspicion, animosity, and envy to go around. As Richler describes it:

> If the Main was a poor man's street, it was also a dividing line. Below [to the east], the French Canadians. Above, some distance above, the dreaded WASPs....

The ghetto in between was the buffer zone. As in the manner of rival poor communities everywhere, the Jews and the French did not get along. Among the French, as Richler has documented, there existed a tradition of anti-Semitism. To the denizens of the ghetto, on the other hand, the French were the goyim, the others, with a different God, who lived and ate according to different rules, with whom intermixing was impossible.

> We fought the French Canadians stereotype for stereotype. If many of them believed that the St. Urbain Street Jews were secretly rich, manipulating the black market, then my typical French Canadian was a moronic gum-chewer. He wore his greasy black hair parted down the middle and also affected an eyebrow moustache.... He was the dolt who held up your uncle endlessly at the liquor

commission while he tried unsuccessfully to add
three figures....

Mordecai Richler was not one for pulling punches. Even
as he concedes that the French "were not entirely unloved"
and that "the real trouble was there was no dialogue between
us and the French Canadians," one can almost sense the
former St. Urbain kid rolling up his sleeves, pitching back
the Jews' replies to the taunts they endured. The wounds of
prejudice are not easily shrugged off. The exiles of the
pogroms who were soon to welcome exiles of the Holocaust
were always quick to spot—or suspect—anti-Semitism.

If the French were "our enemies," the "pea-soups," and
"our schvartzes" (blacks), he adds, it was "only the WASPs
who were truly hated and feared.... It was, we felt, their
country.... [B]ring down the most insignificant, pinched
WASP fire insurance inspector and even the most arrogant
merchant on the street would dip into the drawer for a ten
spot or a bottle and bow and say, 'Sir.'"

"Their country." How telling. And how far young
Mordecai of St. Urbain Street had come when he wrote this,
how far young Canada had come. Anti-Semitism might have
existed at the street level, among the poor. But it was at the
level of haughty discrimination at public places such as the
beaches, clubs, and restaurants that it stung. The Jewish

insecurity and self-consciousness about their humble origins was not easily shaken off; as many would attest to this day, "it never goes away." This would be a recurrent theme in Richler's fiction, as indeed of other Jewish writers of his generation in Canada and the United States.

MORDECAI'S FATHER, Moses Isaac Richler, known as Moe, was the oldest of fourteen children, the only one born in the Old Country, from where he had been brought as an infant. He was not a successful man.

> He worked ... for my fierce, hot-tempered grandfather and a pompous younger brother. Uncle Solly, who had been to high school, had been made a partner in the [scrap] yard, but not my father, the firstborn. He was a mere employee, working for a salary, which fed my mother's wrath. Younger brothers, determined to escape an overbearing father, had slipped free to form their own business, but my father was too timid to join them.

He would be remembered by his son as being short, stout, and fleshy, with a shiny bald head and the floppy Richler ears, though like Mordecai he was slim when young. Moe lived on perpetual hopes for the future, with ready excuses for his failures that even his son learned to mock. A mild-mannered man afraid of his own father, he made attempts at sternness that had little effect on a rebellious Mordecai. His brothers, successful in their own businesses, humoured him and sometimes let him work for them. His wife, Leah (Lily) Rosenberg, scorned him and nagged him to do better.

But Leah had doted on her own father in his lifetime and worshipped his memory after his death in 1935. Mordecai was four at the time; what he could recall of that old grandfather in rabbi's black garb, with flowing grey beard and Eastern features, was sitting on his lap once and drawing a man riding a horse, the man wearing a wide-brimmed hat. A Hasid of the Old Country. Throughout his childhood the boy must have heard enough praises about his mother's father, the great rabbi, "a lion of a man ... a king of Israel," to want to shut him off from his mind. Still, although he hardly made anything of it until much later in his life, the fact remains that he came from an illustrious rabbinical pedigree. And he was not the first writer in the family.

Both Jehudah Rosenberg and his second wife, Sarah Gitel (the first wife had died), came from a long line of Hasidic rabbis, in her case tracing their origins to the disciples of the mystic Baal Shem Tov. For Orthodox Jews, Rabbi Rosenberg's name was one to contend with. Among his scholarly achievements, besides the dry treatises on law and traditional medicine, was a translation, from Aramaic into Hebrew, of the Zohar, a mystical commentary on the Torah. The creative and mystical were evidently his métier. He was also the author, in Hebrew, of a version of the famous legend of the Golem of Prague, an English translation of which is in print. In that story, the golem, a Frankenstein's monster–like creature, saves the Jews of Prague from an outbreak of anti-Semitism.

In 1912 Jehudah Rosenberg had become one of the thousands who left Poland to settle in North America. He came to Toronto. A year later he was followed by his wife and a brood consisting of the five youngest children; two older boys stayed behind. The rabbi already had four children from his first marriage. Leah, born in Poland, was Sarah's sixth child. After living in the Jewish neighbourhood of Toronto's Kensington area for a few years, in 1919 the family headed for the better rabbinical pastures of Montreal.

Evidently, in Moses Richler, hapless son of a scrap dealer, Leah had married the wrong man, and she appreciated neither his excuses for himself nor the practical jokes that he liked to make, perhaps to try to win her. The marriage had been arranged by her father. She loved him but never forgave him for that. During the Depression, times were hard for the couple, and according to Lily her family helped her out with food parcels and cash. She was also more educated than Moe, although she had not been allowed to finish high school. She read Keats and Shelley, and popular novels such as *King's Row* by Henry Bellamann and *The Good Earth* by Pearl Buck. She craved culture and a better life, and even wrote stories, based on life in her father's home. On the other hand, simple Moses assiduously read the *New York Daily Mirror,* especially for the views of the outspoken and fiercely anti-Hitler Walter Winchell, and "devoured" *Popular Mechanics, Doc Savage,* and *Black Mask.* He did not know Beethoven from Bartók.

The boy Mordecai attended one of the Jewish parochial schools of the neighbourhood, called the Talmud Torah, where he studied English, French, and modern Hebrew. Two days a week after school the boys repaired to the backroom of the Young Israel Synagogue for Talmud studies. There, Mr. Yalofsky, the young teacher, might begin by demonstrating to these New World boys some of the finer points of Jewish law that had tested the wisest of the old rabbis.

—If a man tumbles off the roof of an eight-story building and four stories down another man sticks a sword out of the window and stabs him, is that second man guilty of murder? Or not?

—Rabbi Menasha asks, did he fall or was he pushed off the roof?

—Rabbi Yedhua asks, was he already dead of heart failure before he was stabbed?

—Were the two men related?

—Enemies?

—Friends?

"Who cared?" asks the older Mordecai Richler many years later. "Concealed on our laps, below the table, at the risk of having our ears twisted by Mr. Yalofsky, was the *Herald,* opened at the sports pages." The boy, whose mother must have hoped he would become a rabbi one day and keep alive the tradition of her father, was on his way to becoming a modern agnostic and simply a writer. But those lessons from Mr. Yalofsky's class were not in vain; they would remain indelible in Mordecai's mind, and he would go on to extend them with his own readings and research. His knowledge of the Jewish tradition, as demonstrated in his novels, would be impressive. The English teachers, too, left a mark on the boy; from them he learned of Hemingway's Spain and Steinbeck's California, imbibed socialist ideas, and heard the anarchist labourer Sacco's speech to the Massachusetts court.

When Mordecai was thirteen, his parents' marriage finally ended. His mother had become "enthralled" with one of the

German Jewish refugees of the war; these new Jews of Western Europe were the sophisticated lot, not "timorous innocents out of the shtetl." They spoke better English, besides German and French, and took an interest in opera and literature; they would not be caught sitting rapt like Moses Richler before Lili St. Cyr as she simulated intercourse with a swan on the stage of the Gayety. The refugee that Mrs. Richler fell in love with was the boarder the family kept in the spare bedroom to earn extra money. His name was Julius Frenkel.

A divorce in Quebec would have required parliamentary approval, a costly process. And so a loophole was found, and the marriage was annulled in the Quebec court on the false grounds that Lily Richler had married when underage and without her father's approval. I'm a bastard, the boy bragged to his friends, this being his solace for the very obvious pain and embarrassment of the broken home. He stayed with his mother and saw his father mostly on weekends, Moe having agreed to pay $28 monthly to Lily for Mordecai's care. His older brother Avrum was in university, at Queen's, in Kingston.

Though a typical teenager—"I embarrassed him. I got into trouble"—Mordecai developed a bond with his father that tightened over the years. For while Lily, whom Julius Frankel never married, worried about Mordecai's education and fuelled his ambition, filling his ears with talk of culture and eulogies of her father the rabbi, Moses was the simple friend who demanded nothing and was always available with earthy, common-sense, manly advice, a person easy to talk to, who took him to the Richler family gatherings and the synagogue. Who told jokes.

> "Hey, do you know why we eat hard-boiled eggs dipped in salt water just before the Passover meal?"
>
> "No, Daddy. Why?"
>
> "To remind us that when the Jews crossed the Red Sea they certainly got their balls soaked."

After parochial school, Mordecai attended Baron Byng High School, a yellow-brick structure on St. Urbain Street, which in his fiction became transformed into Fletcher's Field High School. It possessed the grim external look of a penitentiary; nevertheless, it was for the boys the heart of the ghetto. Almost all the pupils were from Jewish working-class families of the neighbourhood, those from well-heeled Outremont attending Strathcona Academy; interaction between the two groups was minimal. The Baron Byng parents may have worked at humble and menial jobs, but they well knew that education was the way out of poverty and were therefore fiercely competitive about their kids' education. It was not marks but ranking that mattered, Richler tells us, and being number two meant that there was someone else, the bragging Mrs. Kauffman's kid, perhaps, who was number one. "On St. Urbain Street, a head start was all. Our mothers read us stories from *Life* about pimply astigmatic fourteen-year-olds who had already graduated from Harvard or who were confounding professors at MIT."

The Jewish Public Library in the area was well attended and organized readings and lectures. The *Kanader Adler,* Montreal's daily Yiddish paper established in 1907, brought local and world news besides promoting Yiddish culture. It was what the *zeyda* (grandfather) Shmarya read, sitting in his balcony, overlooking the street. Its English-language version was the *Jewish Daily Eagle.* Yiddish theatre was active in the city, and in the delis and pubs of the Main, world events were followed closely. Not surprisingly, politics in the ghetto followed a leftish bent.

Thirteen-year-olds entering Baron Byng were told by their teachers to work hard, especially if they desired to go on to the city's prestigious McGill University. Entrance to McGill required an average mark of sixty-five for graduating high-schoolers, but the Jews had special consideration: they needed seventy-five. Whether this was official policy or not, it was common knowledge, and the practice lasted well into the 1960s. Their counterparts in the ghettos of the American cities, of course, faced similar obstacles to get into the elite Ivy League colleges. The boys already knew that, and Baron Byng consistently outperformed most, and perhaps all, other schools in Quebec. Taking in through its doors the uncouth sons of plumbers, peddlers, and factory workers, Baron Byng magically produced future doctors, lawyers, scientists, philanthropists, and community leaders. Among its graduates it would later boast a Nobel Prize winner, Rudolph A. Marcus; two of Canada's leading poets, A.M. Klein and Irving Layton; a leading politician, David Lewis; actor William Shatner; and writer Mordecai Richler. Toronto's Jack Rabinovitch, founder of the Scotiabank Giller Prize, also graduated from this school.

Mordecai Richler would describe himself at thirteen as short for his age and pimply. He is remembered as awkward with girls, bookish, and a loner. Different from the rest even then, he would go to basketball games sometimes with a profound-looking tome in his hand, such as H.G. Wells's *Outline of History;* a librarian convinced him to read *All Quiet on the Western Front,* a novel about a young German in the trenches of the First World War, which he enjoyed and where he learned that latkes were also German. Even if he would later boast that he had read only trivial books as a boy, these examples show an exceptional sensibility. He was, one might say, a boy with an attitude: a smart aleck not afraid to speak up, even to his teachers. And as a scion of famous rabbinical scholars, he stood out for his articulation, his writing abilities, and his sheer arrogance. He was also a good artist as a child, and Lily enrolled him in an art class. If one were to go by remembered accounts of him, even taking into account distorted and jaundiced memories, he seems to have been respected by his contemporaries but was not high up in the popularity contest.

His mother had ambitions for him as a rabbi, the traditional vocation a couple of her own brothers had already followed. But Mordecai knew from early on that he wanted to be a writer. Always perfect English, always taking notes, by far the best writer his teachers knew. That is how he is remembered.

THE RICHLERS had traditionally followed the Chabad-Lubavitch branch of the Hasidic movement. Shmarya Richler, the *zeyda,* had after his arrival set himself up in the scrap metal business. Stern and dictatorial in all matters, he demanded strict observance in religion and ritual from his family; young Mordecai was the rebel in the brood, harbinger in the old man's fearful, angry eyes of his precious world's coming end—all that the Eastern Jews had struggled to keep, had brought with them. The battles between the two emblematize a contest between their different worlds. Shmarya, too, was a small man, with a dome head, a beard, and a pinched face; in the writer's description of their tussles, however, he takes on a titanic aspect. There was a *shul* (synagogue) around the corner from St. Urbain where the family went for evening prayers. One day Mordecai and his young uncle Yankel, playing with a chemistry set in the basement, failed to appear at *shul*. On his return, Grandfather Richler "descended on us, seething, his face bleeding red. One by one he smashed our test tubes and our retorts and even our cherished water distiller against the stone wall. Yankel begged forgiveness, but not me." A few days later, continuing his rebellion, Mordecai blackened Yankel's eye. Grandfather summoned Mordecai to his study and thrashed him with his belt.

But "vengeance was mine," says the writer, slightly blasphemously. That vengeance consisted of discovering Shmarya cheating on the scrapyard scales once, thus reducing him pitifully in estimation. Before, he had been stern, cruel, perhaps righteous. And now? "Scornful, triumphant, I ran to my father and told him his father was no better than a cheat and a hypocrite.

"What do you know?" my father demanded.

"Nothing."

"They're anti-Semites, every one of them."

The short-changed peddler happened to be a drunken Irishman.

Mordecai resisted wearing the yarmulke, would not keep the Sabbath. When he told his father he was an atheist, having read about Charles Darwin, Moe told him simply to put his yarmulke on or he would cut off his allowance. The boy complied; he had only been testing. One Sunday afternoon, visiting the *zeyda* with his father, not having been to *shul* the previous evening, which was the Sabbath, he found Shmarya waiting for him. Before the entire family, denouncing him as a Sabbath goy, his grandfather pulled him by the ear, slapped him about the face, and threw him out of the house. The two never spoke again.

It is a remarkable relationship, between a rigid, tyrannical Orthodox patriarch from the shtetl who controlled the entire family and the rebel grandson who broke away to become a secular and outspoken writer. As far as we can tell they never got to understand each other at the time. But many years later, when Mordecai was closer in age to his grandfather, he would take time to cast a sympathetic eye on poor Shmarya.

Shmarya Richler died when Mordecai was fourteen. When Mordecai went to the house on Jeanne Mance Street to attend the funeral, the coffin had been set on the living room floor, the grieving aunts and uncles gathered around. One of the uncles cornered the teenager as he entered, barring his way, we imagine, and told him, "You hastened his death ... you are not a good Jew ... don't you dare touch his coffin!"

That was the instruction the old man had left in his will, his final punishment of the rebel. Mordecai was not to touch his coffin. Mordecai turned to his father. Help me, help me, he pleaded silently.

And so the rebellion, the breaking away, was not easy. It never is.

AT THE DEATH OF HIS FATHER, in 1967, Mordecai Richler wrote a moving tribute to that erstwhile loser; he wrote of how the two had become closer over the years. He missed him, he would say, in a rare display of open emotion. In Richler's fiction, Moe appears in various guises, always down-to-earth, always likeable. Even in the guise of a mobster's enforcer, there is that goodness to him, a certain gentleness. Not so Lily. Richler never wrote anything approaching a tribute to his mother, always mentioning her in relation to Moe, and he acknowledged her father, Jehudah, whom she worshipped, only in his later years. In his fiction she is not a likeable character. In life she was a hard and bitter woman, out of place in her milieu, often aloof; she has not been remembered well by almost everyone, including her two sons. But she doted on Mordecai.

The hurt in his childhood—his parents' divorce—would have been ameliorated by the closeness of the community in which Richler grew up. There was the synagogue, the school, the Talmud Torah, the clamorous life of the street with its vibrant oral culture and robust sense of humour. There were aunts and uncles and their numerous offspring; there were births and deaths, anniversaries and festivals. At his own bar mitzvah he performed brilliantly. At such close quarters, and with such large families, naturally there were conflicts, many of them bitter. People could not but reveal themselves. Everyone knew everyone else, heard secrets and rumours.

He would return to this communal set-up repeatedly in his fiction and essays. From it he would derive his moral outlook. Specifically, the major influences on his life include his relationships with his two grandfathers—one of them dead but famous and revered, living on in his mother's memory to an oppressive degree; the other authoritarian and a bully, pious but, in his grandson's eyes, a cheat. There was then the trauma of his parents' quarrels, his mother's treatment of her husband, her extramarital affair, which was his humiliation, and the couple's ultimate divorce. Life on the street and in the school among other Canadian kids would have been fun. But the attitudes of the adults, especially his grandfather Shmarya and his mother, Lily, despite all the professions of piety and tradition, were hypocritical, a lie. Perhaps this was too harsh a judgment, but from it undoubtedly he acquired his hatred of hypocrisy and double-talk. More and more, in the positions he took in his later years, it was the simple honesty and unpretentiousness of his father, Moe, that he leaned toward.

IN THE SUMMER OF 1948, one day there came in the mail his final report from Baron Byng High School: a depressing 64.6 percent. Algebra and French had done him in. (The fact that marks from so long back are remembered reflects a culture that was academically competitive and traditionally respectful of scholarship.) He did reasonably in English, well in history. Mordecai Richler would not have been admitted to McGill even had he not been a Jew. He did not even apply. He entered Sir George Williams College (SGW), run by the YMCA, instead. Within days of his admission he was a reporter for the students' weekly, the *Georgian,* one of the few with his own byline. "Emancipation Hop Riotous Success:

Annual Freshman Frolic Sparked by Westernaires" was the headline of one of his first reports, in the October 14, 1948, issue. Three weeks later he wrote an enthusiastic feature on Israel: "A People Come Home!" By the following year, his name appeared on the masthead as the day editor. And he had already become controversial, winning opprobrium or approval from *Georgian* readers.

"Drama Guild Presentation Proves Mediocre" ran the December 1949 headline of his damning review of *Out of the Frying Pan.*

> It is difficult enough to review a play when you will never have to face the cast again, unless by way of an accidental meeting. But when it is a critic's duty to pan a production in spite of the fact that he will doubtless have to meet the cast from day to day, and exchange meaningless "hellos" and weather comments with the group, things are apt to prove rather unpleasant....
>
> Perhaps, the most admirable thing about the production were the usherettes, and the programme, both of whom were very well designed.

The editor thought it fit to note at the end, tongue in cheek, that "M.R. will be very scarce around the College these next few weeks."

Mordecai Richler was enjoying himself writing.

A few weeks later, in February 1950, he wrote a much more provocative editorial against the recognition of the Hillel Society as an official group at the college.

> The recognition of this group would not only mean toleration—*but active endorsement*—of religious segregation on our campus.
>
> In theory Hillel claims its membership is open to Christians, Moslems, Witnesses of Jehovah, and what have you, but in practice the whole concept of an "open membership" Hillel is meaningless.

Letters of protest poured in, addressed to the editor: "It seems M.R., the cantankerous embryo, boy genius of the 'High News' has caused some new annoyance in his inability to furnish with civility the more intelligent objections to Hillel recognition," wrote one piqued correspondent. Another opined with sarcasm that perhaps the "M.R." who signed the editorial was not Mordecai Richler but "Moishe Rebaynim (known to Goyim as Moses) himself … returned to lead the Jews.… Even if the lowly Mordecai … did write the controversial column, I propose it be inscribed on twin tablets and hung on the notice board." Another writer, "Son of Israel," however, approved of M.R.

Mordecai Richler had begun to engage the Jews.

He did not think much of the curriculum at Sir George, wrote contemptuously of it in his later years, and his grades there reflected his disengagement from it. He believed there was a Jewish quota at the college, a proposition affirmed to him indirectly by a faculty member over a drink. Still, those were basically years of fun, when his education outside of the ghetto began. It was at Sir George where he made his first gentile friends. Terry introduced him to opera; Phil to the poets Eliot, cummings, and Auden; surprisingly, as he put it, "I had never heard of any of them before." Stuart was inspirational—he signed up on a ship headed for the West Indies.

On the one hand, drinking was what college education was about—drinking and retching. On the other, "new, mostly literary, worlds" were opening up for him: it was an exhilarating experience. And "when we weren't drinking, or arguing about Kafka or Thurber, both sacrosanct, we were at the afternoon movies."

> There were the Marx Brothers revivals and the new Montgomery Clift film, Virginia Mayo doing Dana Andrews dirty in *The Best Years of Our Lives,* Robert Ryan in *The Set-Up* and Rita Hayworth of blessed memory peeling off her gloves in *Gilda....* We read *Partisan Review, Commentary,* and the

New Yorker, and the writers who excited us were Truman Capote, Carson McCullers, S.J. Perelman, Norman Mailer, Tennessee Williams, Graham Greene, and Jean-Paul Sartre.

As did Hemingway, Scott Fitzgerald, Dylan Thomas.

He wangled a job at the *Montreal Herald,* for which he covered college basketball games and amateur theatricals. Once he went as a critic to the famous Gayety Theatre, where the legendary Lili St. Cyr had performed. The stripper whom he interviewed, however, was one Candy Parker. The only Canadian writer who excited these young people was Morley Callaghan, who had sat with Hemingway and Fitzgerald at the Dôme in Montparnasse, Paris.

But there was already a literary group in the city, consisting of older writers and hopefuls, dedicated to a kind of writing that was more reflective of their experience as Canadians. It was associated with the *Northern Review,* a little magazine edited by John Sutherland, and included both Irving Layton and Louis Dudek. Later they were joined by Phyllis Webb and Leonard Cohen. Richler came to know Sutherland, how well is not clear (he "fell in" with him is how he put it), but to the older avant-gardists the nineteen-year-old recent arrival from the ghetto and Baron Byng, though a genius to his mother and his classmates, must have seemed callow and naïve and he perhaps embarrassed himself. He also hung around a college bar called the Shrine with a crowd of potential writers, according to one of whom, "Mordecai was a little kid, hanging around. He was raw, very raw, very brash."

Which is exactly what Sutherland told Mavis Gallant when—as she relates it—she asked him about Richler: "What's he like?" Sutherland replied, "He's very brash. Everything goes through his head, he's a know-all."

The early Richler seemed to create such an impression. None of the older literary crowd could know that the kid elbowing himself into their midst was not just a dreamer or a talker but absolutely serious about his writing. And he in turn found the literary scene in Canada mediocre and wanting. Perhaps this was a natural reaction to being overlooked or dismissed. But he would not wait to be admitted into this pond; he would rather go out into the world of real writers and prove himself.

It has been suggested that he was asked not to return to Sir George after his second year due to his having written offensive articles in the *Georgian*. Certainly, an anonymous report, titled "Nite-Cap: a blemish on college due to closeness: one reporter's view," had been published about the notorious Nite-Cap Café during his watch as the day editor;

the café, recommended by taxi drivers and cops alike, was used as a pickup place for prostitutes. It is also possible that Richler left the college because he did not get the post of *Georgian* editor-in-chief, the money from which would have paid his school expenses. Whatever the trigger for his departure, there was nothing to keep him at Sir George if he wanted to become a serious writer like Hemingway, Scott Fitzgerald, or Callaghan. One day in 1950, he and his friend Terry from the *Georgian* walked into Thomas Cook's travel agency and bought one-way steamship tickets for Liverpool. They departed in September.

CHAPTER THREE

Out in the World

Mordecai's friend Ed Koch describes meeting him in France a few years after the former had left home to be a writer:

> ... I went to the south of France. Mordecai was living in a village.... We drank in the town's only bar, a café with tables set up in the town's small square. Mordecai was taciturn, watchful, rabbinical. I did most of the talking. There was not much indication of the wit that he possessed, though at one point he asked me who my favourite novelist was. I answered, somewhat pretentiously, "Henry James." "Then you'll be right at home with my novels, won't you?" We chuckled and kept drinking.

It is a precious picture of the writer as young man, out in the world alone, uncertain; a contrast with what others had seen as the brash young pup, overconfident. This was the private Mordecai.

MUCH AS THE MONTREAL of the 1940s and 1950s has been described as a lively and exciting city, it was still a backwater compared with the great metropolises of London, Paris, and New York. These centres defined the cultural and political beat of the times; consequently their attraction for the young man or woman out in the colonies or backwaters anywhere was enormous.

In Europe lay the romance of the bohemian: the young artist as revolutionary. Paris, the City of Lights, in particular, was still the cultural capital of the Western world, the spiritual home of the painter, musician, and writer, its name associated with a seemingly endless list of intellectual and artistic luminaries of the past. In the 1920s it had attracted a number of literary expatriates, dubbed "the Lost Generation" by Gertrude Stein, for they had come of age during the First World War. They had included Hemingway, Fitzgerald, and Dos Passos. Joyce and Pound might also be found in the city in the 1920s and, later, Beckett. All of them were of iconic status by the 1950s, having left a trail of artistic genius, exile, and freedom.

In the 1950s, while the United States lay in the grip of unbending McCarthyism, a new wave of North American émigrés appeared in Paris, inspired partly by that earlier generation of cultural superstars. While the previous generation had patronized the cafés of Montparnasse, the 1950s crowd took their leisure at the cafés of the Left Bank and Saint-Germain-des-Prés. Here in the cafés—the Mabillon and Les Deux Magots the better known among them—the urgent questions of art, existence, and world revolution found expression; in the streets outside you could run into Sartre or Camus, Beckett or Malraux. The world's exiles too found in Paris a congenial home; and Hollywood, not to be left behind, found it a profitable setting.

In 1951 Gene Kelly and Leslie Caron danced to Gershwin's music in *An American in Paris.* Albert Camus, already the author of *The Myth of Sisyphus* and *The Stranger,* published *The Rebel* that same year. A rift between Camus and Sartre set Paris abuzz. Beckett's *Watt* and *Molloy* and Nabokov's *Lolita* were all published in early 1950s Paris. *Waiting for Godot* premiered there in 1953, and then the rest of the world got to see it.

For this romantic yet artistically exciting world, Mordecai Richler, as he was to write later in *Home Sweet Home: My Canadian Album,* "sailed away from Canada without regrets."

His first letter to his father was written on board the RMS *Franconia.* He had caught a cold, he said, and had become seasick twice. They docked at Liverpool, from where he took a train to London. He stayed there for a week, and then on a lovely Paris autumn afternoon emerged at the Saint-Germain-des-Prés Métro station, "exhilarated beyond compare." London was not half the city Paris was, he wrote to Dad. He had found a room on the Rue Cujas, 5th Arrondissement, and planned to make his own breakfast and dinner. Meanwhile, could he get a food parcel? Immediately having moved in, he hurried over to a café and sat outside at a table with a notebook and pen, doing his best, he would mock himself many years later, to look writerly. He was being cruel to himself, surely; what writer, young or old, would not wish to note down his first impressions of Paris? But wearing a blue beret as he sat there pensively was perhaps overdoing it.

It was a grubby, penurious existence he lived, the type many a foreign student or apprentice can attest to in a foreign city: cold and hungry nights inside dingy, dark apartments, skimping on food and clothing (even on underwear, he once said), awaiting food parcels and money from home, borrowing from fellow exiles, in his case those from North America. Mavis Gallant, a little older than he was and having preceded him in Paris, describes going to visit him once during those early months.

> … I bought some fruit and whatever you take to
> someone from Canada who is dying of flu. I

remember going up a very dark staircase that frightened me. It was an unheated room on a court. I knocked and he had a toque or hockey cap pulled down over his head, and he had on scarves and a sweater and he was sitting up in bed reading from the light of the window....

But this was his own life, hardships and all, an adventure and a discovery; he was meeting new young people, ideas came pouring into the mind, and he was writing all the time. He continued to read voraciously, completing his literary education. Gallant had caught him with a copy of Robert Herrick; he also soaked himself in Malraux, Céline, Sartre, Camus, Hemingway.

He wrote regularly to Moe and Lily. From Moe, he received $50 every month, from Lily, $20. This seems to be what had been promised to him. From both he received regular food parcels and that much-beloved item, cigarettes. Sometimes he requested typewriter ribbons for his Royal portable, which Moe had bought for him before he left. There seems to have been an understanding that Mordecai would pay back his father upon his return, after a two-year absence. Moe's letters are good-natured, not overly long, with news from home; sometimes he sent magazines. He was not doing well but came up with the money every month. Mordecai's "Dear Daddy" letters were often brisk, with reports about his work, and requests—rather, demands—for the money, in the manner of any twenty-year-old abroad. The operative word seemed to have been *pronto,* and he had taken on the affectation of using only lower case:

> about the next parcel. i would appreciate it if on dec. 25th, not earlier, not later, you would mail me another parcel to cambridge, eng. [where he would be spending a few days with a friend]
>
> [signed] mutty

He was not above manipulating or bullying the gentle Moe: "i got my mother's parcel all right." "… i'm counting on you! my mother has also sent money … Mordy." And "my mother will continue to send $20 a month."

Mentions of Lily are important to take note, for whereas Moe's letters have been preserved from the time of Mordecai's departure for Europe on the *Franconia* right until his father's death, Lily's early letters are absent from the archives he deposited. Perhaps they were culled because of the painful falling-out later of mother and son. That would be a pity, for those letters, which must have arrived with the money and the parcels, were no doubt as long and detailed as her later, preserved correspondence and would have revealed the relationship between the two at that early stage in Mordecai Richler's career.

There existed a lively and closely linked expatriate community in Paris that included would-be writers and publishers of small magazines and presses, many of them Americans. In December 1950 there arrived in Paris another Montrealer, recently fired from the *Gazette,* now a freelance journalist and prospective writer. He was twenty-five and already known to Mavis Gallant, who had quit her job at the same newspaper to come to Paris and write, and who introduced him to Mordecai Richler. He is young and is determined to be a writer, Gallant told him. During the next few days the three of them hit the fashionable night spots of Saint-Germain-des-Prés, the Latin Quarter, and Montparnasse. Writes William Weintraub:

> We were all writing, or pretending to write, but at the cocktail hour some of us would gather, for Pernods or *fines à l'eau,* with a growing tribe of expatriates. On prosperous days it would be the Deux Magots, on thin days it would be the Mabillon. If a cheque arrived in the mail, there was the possibility of dinner at the Brasserie Lipp or in the ancient rooms of the Procope, where

Voltaire used to dine. Other times it was in the dim little student restaurants. It was the golden age of the Left Bank and in its watering holes we were on the alert to catch sight of Jean-Paul Sartre, Jacques Prévert, Albert Camus, Juliette Greco.

Richler continued to create the impression in his older friends and acquaintances of a brash know-all, pushy but single-minded. It is easy to forget, reading these recollections, that he was a teenager still; they were all young, but he might well have been the youngest and perhaps was often merely tolerated. They thought of him as someone who *wanted* to be a writer, that is, who had dreams or boasted or was naïve. What did he know? Legions came to Paris claiming to write or become artists. Thus, Weintraub to his friend Brian Moore:

> Did I tell you about this Richler? He's from Montreal, has a peculiar first name—Mordecai— and wants to be a writer. Very young and rather cheeky, without proper deference when dealing with older citizens like myself.

But after the partying and hanging around in cafés, back in his dank room, the youngster exhausted himself at his typewriter. He wrote short pieces that he sent off, receiving rejections, and he was working on a novel. Little did his new acquaintances know the private demons he was wrestling at the time, which would find their place in the novels and in a manner define him. As Richler himself would admit, they never discussed "our stuff," or admitted "that we laboured long and hard in our hotel rooms, real Americans after all, shoulders to the wheel, determined to make our mark." Among them were Terry Southern and James Baldwin; Mavis Gallant was already sending off her first stories to *The New Yorker*. William Weintraub, as he wandered about Europe on his sabbatical, dispatched journalistic pieces back to Canada.

Mordecai Richler and William Weintraub began a close friendship during those months, despite the difference in age and experience between them, and when the latter regretfully returned to Montreal eight months later (he had had a good time, but by his own admission his dedication to art did not extend to be "willing to scrape by in abject poverty, living on borrowed pittances, sleeping on someone's floor and desperately waiting for that cheque from home"), the two continued a correspondence that lasted into the 1970s. Weintraub, moreover, had financial means in Montreal, and he seems to have been exceptionally generous, on several occasions coming to Richler's timely assistance with emergency funds.

Before Weintraub departed for Montreal, on April 1, 1951, a surprising letter arrived from his new friend Mordecai Richler from, of all places, an island off Barcelona in the Mediterranean called Ibiza. "DEAR BILL:" the letter began,

> i am broke and i'm not broke, a rather curious position to be in.... mavis said—god bless you— you might be able to lend me a few bucks until sept.—if so, fine if not, i know the type!... if you ... can spare $25 or $50 until sept. or oct. to say i would appreciate the whole thing would be putting it mildly....

This was perhaps the first time Richler ventured to ask Weintraub for a loan. There was also an invitation to come to visit. Mordecai was hoping Mavis would be willing to share the house he had rented in a village called San Antonio on Ibiza. But Mavis was not around. Weintraub went to consult a map to look up Ibiza.

Richler had gone to Spain for a cheap place in the sun where he could write, perhaps also to escape the chattering, partying expatriate crowd of Paris; one could, after all, talk oneself silly and be left with nothing to write, or become plagued by doubts. A writer needs to be lonely. Moreover, Spain occupied a rather special and romantic place in his youthful mythology: it was where the Republicans had fought the Fascists in the civil war of the 1930s, all the good men on the side of the former; a war to which many idealistic young men of the time from many nations had gone to fight on the good side and which Hemingway had used as a setting for his novel *For Whom the Bell Tolls.*

The three-bedroom house Richler rented on the island was far more comfortable than the rooms in Paris; it came with a cook. And he was treated royally by the local men, who assumed he was a runaway from the Korean War. Food was cheap, as was alcohol; wine was delivered on the doorstep every morning instead of milk. Then there was the brothel at Rosita's, where the men would creep off in the dark, in secrecy (they hoped) from their wives. The fishermen all hung out at the Bar Escandell, and this, too, became Richler's watering hole and his postal address. His wavy hair was long and he sported a light beard; small and dark, he could have been taken for a Spaniard.

There was a jetty on the island where folks would go to greet the odd boat coming in from the mainland. It would have been the highlight of the day. On one such vessel arrived a beautiful, dark-haired American girl called Helen, accompanied by her mother. She stayed on the island for some weeks, during which she and Mordecai became lovers.

On another boat one morning arrived William Weintraub. He spent a few weeks. On a typical day that he describes, the two would spend all morning at their typewriters, then go for swims in the afternoons and repair to the Escandell for drinks.

Richler's youthful letters to friends regarding life in Paris and Spain might suggest a debauched existence, but one suspects a good deal of it was boasting or mere highlighting. Richler was an obsessive writer; nothing else mattered more. Thus, a letter to Dad from Ibiza:

> im very tired. its just about six pm and im knocking this letter off after a hard afternoon of working in a bastard heat....
> ... Pops—abt the money....

He was desperately trying to finish a long first novel.

Spain, Ibiza, was a profound experience and rite of passage. He had time to write and think, to be alone. He lived among a simple people surviving modestly, whom he did not have to impress with his ambitions, who seem to have taken him seriously. He also had some intriguing experiences, which not only provided him material for the work of first fiction at hand, but also were profound and unforgettable enough for him to return to in a subsequent novel many years later. It was less than a year since he had left home.

When William Weintraub returned to Montreal, Lily naturally wanted news about her son. Did he drink too much? What was this Helen like? Weintraub, reporting positively, put Lily's fears at rest, and earned a dinner at her home in gratitude. She was very much in Mordecai's life. Previously, when Mordecai wrote to her about Helen, she had replied asking if he was using contraceptives. It was advice Mordecai had already received from Moe on the eve of his departure from Montreal.

To Daddy, a request from Ibiza:

> here's what I would like you to send me pronto in
> a parcel.
>   1. a camera (please) …
>   2. three typewriter ribbons. black. royal portable.
>   3. two clip on bowties. they are for friends.

Kindly, accommodating Moe must have questioned finally the wisdom of indulging his son on hard-earned money. Other young men Mordecai's age were already working, or in university training to be doctors and lawyers. Couldn't Mordecai have stayed in Montreal and worked while writing his bestseller? Mordecai had, in fact, worked with his uncles for a few months before he left, earning more money than Moe. Now here he was, on the one hand starving, on the other, travelling to England, Italy, Algiers, of all places, and now he was on some backward island in Spain.

One day, Moe wrote a harsh letter to his son, threatening to cut off funds. It must have taken some thought and desperation on his part. We have Mordecai's reply to guide us about the "misunderstanding," as he called it.

> if you don't continue to send me the $50 monthly until sept. i'm screwed. i have nothing to fall back on here in spain.... if your attitude is <u>still</u> the same as the one in your last letter to me, you may be <u>sure</u> i will never again burden you with my troubles. in fact, if you really feel the way you represented yourself in that letter, we can terminate all relationships in sept.... every bloody cent will be paid back to you some day. now that money, and not me and my work, seem to mean so much to you.
>
> regards to sarah and the kids.
>
> Mutty [by hand]

What is a father to do, with such a meaningless threat from a child? So disturbed was Mordecai, he continued the letter overleaf, writing an afterthought by hand.

my threats may sound feeble in comparison to yours, but if you decide to abandon me, i want you to know that if my book is published—or if not this one, the next one—i want the Richler family to never speak of me, or claim me as a relative simply because i have suddenly acquired fame.

you may think i'm being unfair—but if you have a copy of your letter ... and re-read it, you will see it is you who has been unjust—terribly unjust.

i hope that—for both our peace of mind— your next letter will be more friendly and that our difficulties will [be] resolved.

Think the matter over carefully.

love [almost illegible]

M

His letters to Moe are touching, all the more so when we realize what a tender relationship developed between the two over the years. They provide the needed corrective to the exuberant, boastful letters of the novice writer to his friends, to the character references supplied by them and other more casual acquaintances. In these letters to Moe he is the private Mordecai Richler, son and child, struggling with emotion, survival, family. All the more the pity that letters from this period to and from Lily are unavailable.

Clearly in the above letter Mordecai acknowledges himself as a Richler, a member of the large clan among whom he grew up; and he demonstrates a fear of abandonment. Both factors are significant for someone struggling with, as we shall see, the question of Jewish identity and assimilation.

ONLY A FEW WEEKS LATER Richer ran into a problem and left Ibiza in a hurry. It was early July when he departed for France. The problem was this.

Among the expatriates on the island were a few Germans, including a former SS colonel called Mueller, under death sentence in France but decorated by Franco, a suave and overbearing personality who enjoyed taunting the younger, somewhat intimidated, and unsophisticated Richler. The young man finally one day plucked up the courage to tell the German off in a café. What made matters worse between them was that the pretty Helen had chosen to favour Mordecai instead of Mueller. The German group began a campaign against Richler, informing the local secret policeman that he was a spy. The island was small, which was its attraction, but it could also make a person quickly undesirable. As someone who kept mainly to himself, writing, and who received money from abroad, he was a curious creature on the local scene, anyway. Mueller was a more established figure and a friend of the regime. Told by the local policeman to leave or be deported, Richler left for the south of France. That departure would haunt him; it had been too hasty, he would think, and many years later, a much older man, he would return to confront the scene once again.

He spent time first at Tourrettes-sur-Loup and then Haut-de-Cagnes, both a short distance from Cannes, where he continued work on his novel, banging away feverishly at his typewriter up to ten hours a day. Helen, who was close by in Cannes, would come to see him, and is described as wonderful, just like a wife, gentle and sweet. She cooked for him.

On August 14, 1951, Richler wrote a triumphant, somewhat patronizing letter to his father.

> Dear Dad & Sarah: i finished my novel this morning! cheers and all that. i feel empty and exhausted and clean—never write, old boy, do anything, but never write. dig ditches, make money, build monuments, live and die, bring babies into the world—but don't write. we bleed, boy, we bleed....

He asked for money, and offered to buy for them lovely French stuff—scarves, tablecloths, table napkins.

What did he "bleed" into his first novel? The typescript is called "The Rotten People" and is fairly long, at some four hundred pages. It describes a young man called Kerman Adler who leaves Canada for London, from where he departs for Paris and ends up in Ibiza. On a page of rough notes for the book, the author has written "Knowledge, Guilt, Death, Evil, Pain." These were the existential questions of the day, no less important to a young man for being trendy, and a far cry from "fuckey fuckey" at Rosita's. What comes as a surprise is that, although thus far, judging by available correspondence, Mordecai's Jewishness does not seem to have been an issue, his narrator, Kerman, is obsessed by it:

> [Says Kerman,] "Larkin thinks I'm trying to conceal my being a Jew."
>
> Frank laughed derisively. "I don't think you're trying to conceal it," he said. "In fact you're the most obviously Jewish person I know. You're so damn sensitive to the whole problem that you try your best to minimize it. But actually being a Jew boy torments you so much that you're at the same time a vicious anti-Semite and a typical nauseating

Jewish intellectual. Being a Jew is what has driven
you to Paris, and what is driving you now."

This is where one wishes for a confession from the
author. In its absence one cannot help seeing in the above
passage young Mordecai speaking to a mirror, making a confession of sorts. So much of this first novel is autobiographical. In a letter to Moe he had asked for an English
translation of the Kaddish, a Jewish prayer, to use in the
book. Evidently Kerman is based on Mordecai, and Frank's
charge against Kerman is what Mordecai would himself face
from his detractors in the future.

Elsewhere in the novel, Kerman asks, "But, after all, what
is a Jew?" He goes on to answer the question.

> The Concise Oxford Dictionary ... says, quote,
> "Jew,[1] Person of Hebrew Race; (trans; colloq.)
> extortionate usurer, driver of hard bargains; rich as
> a Jew.; incredulous person; tell that (unlikely tale)
> to the J.; ... J,[2] v.t. (colloq.) cheat, overreach ..."

As we know, Richler's greater novels are studies of this
question in various forms. But it was a secret burden not
shared openly with friends, and his were the doubts he could
not raise with his Orthodox parents. It was in the privacy to

which he had escaped, away from his drinking and cavorting buddies talking literature and art, that he struggled with his Jewish identity.

A doggerel he considered including in the novel ran

> O, Come on you Jews, & hear!
> Why must you wander—
> Wander alone, from scene to scene
> Is to assimilate so obscene?

A current of anxiety then runs through Richler's early life regarding the issue of assimilation and Jewishness; a despair any young man or woman from a closed community might feel facing the larger world and the prospect and thrill of breaking away, as well as the guilt and loneliness that result.

Richler was told by his literary friends in Paris that though he was "young and brilliant," his manuscript "The Rotten People" could not get published because the bourgeois public was not ready for it—the kind of comforting endorsement from friends that can mean anything. He did send it around, without success. Cynically he said that if he were a homosexual, New Directions might just publish it. But he immediately began revising it; that revision, over the next few months, became another novel, which he provisionally called "The Jew of Valencia." He produced it during his second year in Europe, which he spent going back and forth between France and England. He was also anticipating returning to Montreal. Helen was still in his life and they corresponded. She had already had an abortion the previous summer, and he thought he would take her back with him to Canada and marry her. But he also had two other girls in his life: a Swede called Ulla and another girl called Sanki. In March, from England, he asked Moe to send him $200 to book a passage back. By this time he had run up an account of approximately $2,000 with Moe, a considerable sum, for which he sent a carefully prepared statement. He hoped he would not have to pay much more. Moe meanwhile had been having a hard time financially, and his monthly payments to Mordecai had been reduced. But he was now "Zeyda," his older son Avrum having recently become a father. "DEAR GRANDPAPA … MAZEL*TOV," wrote Mordecai from Cambridge and wondered about the kid's name. He spent the following summer in Tourrettes-sur-Loup, close to Helen (in Cannes), though Ulla was with him, and this complicated the matter, as he put it. About Helen he remained ambivalent. He had said he had fallen out of love with her and marriage was off, though not sex. She, on the other hand, was evidently still in love with him. From Tourrettes-sur-Loup, however, he wrote to Weintraub that Helen was coming back to Montreal with him. "Imagine me steering her into Ruby Foo's on Wednesday nights." Ruby Foo's was Montreal's popular kosher Chinese restaurant.

In late August or early September 1952, Richler departed by boat from Liverpool for Canada. He arrived on September 13 in Quebec City, where his brother Avrum met him. He had "a scraggly beard" and came with a large box of books. Helen was not with him.

Richler's relations with women during the two-year sojourn in Europe present an interesting conundrum. We don't know enough. We don't have the women's, especially Helen's, versions of the relationships. There is a certain crudeness in his references to women, though at times he does show qualms as soon as he's typed something awful. Since he was known, only a few years before, to be awkward with girls, can we suppose an element of youthful boastfulness, a macho affectation in his letters to other men at this time? He would be known for his reserve, to the point of absolute silence at a gathering, and was a monogamist and devoted husband and family man the rest of his life, following a failed first marriage; with Helen, at barely twenty-one, he did contemplate marriage and commitment.

HE WROTE TWO NOVELS in two years, the second one, "The Jew of Valencia," becoming *The Acrobats* in its final form. A compact novel, in a style vastly different from the one he would develop in later years, it examines the interactions of a group of émigrés in Valencia, Spain. The main character, insofar as there is one, is a young Canadian painter, André, in the midst of an existential angst. It seems that Richler, after the failure of "The Rotten People" to find takers, had reworked its material to produce the considerably shorter *Acrobats*. This is indicated, for example, by the fact that in the draft manuscripts of the first book, "Kerman" is some-times cancelled and overwritten with "André" by hand. Both young men are in the midst of a crisis; but, perhaps on advice, André is not a Jew. His crisis is simply his failure to connect. Both novels also have in them the snarky German character Roger Kraus, based on the real Mueller.

By the time he reached Montreal from Quebec City, Richler must have shaved off his beard, for his friend Weintraub describes him as clean-shaven. In Montreal he lived with his mother to begin with and found a job with the CBC as a writer for the newsroom, working the evening shift; he also worked for his uncles. He met several people who would turn out to be important in his life. One of them, in Toronto, was the charismatic Ted Allan, who, having served with Norman Bethune in the Spanish Civil War, had just recently co-authored a bestselling biography of

Bethune; Richler left a copy of his manuscript with him. Also in Toronto, he met Robert Weaver of the CBC, a well-known producer of Canadian short stories. And finally, over drinks at the Montreal Press Club, Weintraub introduced Richler to Brian Moore. A long-lasting friendship would develop among the three men; Mavis Gallant, now a resident of Paris, made up the fourth of a peculiarly Montreal literary quartet. Weintraub would remain anchored in Montreal and maintain a closeness with the others of this group. Gallant, on the other hand, did not like Moore very much, and with Richler maintained a distant relationship. And the friendship between Moore and Richler, though warm, carried from the beginning a thin toxic streak that finally overcame it.

In Montreal, Mordecai Richler had met Cathy Boudreau, a young woman with whom he started going out and subsequently, moving out from Lily's, living together. But he was far from settled, in life or in career. It was a nerve-racking time for him. Before he left London, he had left a copy of his manuscript with an agent called Joyce Weiner, who had been introduced to him by a Paris acquaintance. The manuscript was now doing the rounds of publishers in New York and London, and news came from Weiner of one rejection following another.

One day, however, Weiner called to tell him that the London firm of Andre Deutsch wanted to publish the book. They offered a small advance and stipulated some changes. Mordecai Richler was overjoyed. All his self-confidence, his cockiness as others saw it, had been vindicated. He had always believed that among those who were doing the café rounds in Paris, he was the one who had "It." He left the CBC job and started revising the manuscript. And he decided to go back to Europe.

CHAPTER FOUR

An Expatriate in London

In August 1953, elated that he would now be a published novelist at the age of twenty-two, Mordecai Richler crossed the Atlantic on the *Samaria,* ostensibly to promote his novel. So much had happened since he had dropped out of college and left Canada the first time, hardly more than a boy. He was now a man of experience. Those two years away had been his university, and it was a year since he returned. Barring New York, where he had made no headway, it was evident that for him the action was in London. In his decision to return there he showed the typical attribute of the self-exiled, a longing for home and the familiar, and yet an inability to abandon the metropolis. London was the source of his prestige at home, the place where he could further his career. His exile, moreover, gave him a measure of freedom and distance, a sense of perspective that many would argue are vital to a writer. We may be thankful therefore that he returned to Europe, where he developed the distinct voice in which he wrote his great novels. In London, too, Richler could promote himself; his notorious reserve did not extend to the business and networking aspects of his career. Not for him hiding out and letting the work speak for itself. As Moe had advised him once in another context (arguing against university), it is not what you know but who you know. Another piece of Moe's advice would soon be forthcoming: since the title of his first novel began with *A,* why not let his second title begin with *B,* and so on, a whole alphabet series of them? This only gave his son an amusing something to write about him, albeit in the warmest terms.

In Richler's life his companion Cathy's presence is only a little less shadowy than his previous girlfriend Helen's. Cathy was from an English Quebec family, was good-looking in a tall and slender sort of way, and a little older than Mordecai. She has had her detractors among Richler's friends. But, as in the case of Helen, it's impossible to evaluate a private relationship based on second-hand testimony presented decades later. The two certainly seem to have had some fun times together. It has been suggested that she had gone along to London with Mordecai uninvited; that she had a sharp tongue; that she was boring. One feels sorry for her, and inclined to retort, Perhaps she was in the wrong company. She is so thinly represented, and that too, mostly by his friends. Florence Richler, however, remembers her affectionately: "She was feisty, temperamental, much more bohemian than I, a similar sense of humour, very gregarious. I came to enjoy her, and really liked her a lot." Mordecai evidently needed her. Surely there must have been some compatibility.

Upon arrival in London, they rented a basement flat in a very modest part of the city, moving twice within the following few months. Life was hard and Cathy found low-paying work, such as shorthand-typing, to support them. Richler was busy, feverishly writing his next novel, quite absorbed in himself. He liked his drink, though always after a day's work.

But for him now there was the euphoria of being a real writer, associating with other writers, his publisher, his agent. His editor at Deutsch was Diana Athill, who held him in high regard and indulged him a bit, as she did another of her writers from the colonies, V.S. Naipaul. Here is how she saw Richler:

> I liked him very much, but sometimes found myself asking, "Why?", because he hardly ever spoke: I have never known anyone else so utterly unequipped with small-talk as he was then. How could one tell that someone was generous, kind, honest and capable of being very funny if he

hardly ever said a word? I still don't know how but it happened....

What a contrast with his chummy correspondence with William Weintraub and Brian Moore. The person who wrote, as many readers often discovered, was not the man they met in person.

One day, however, he wrote a rather uncharacteristically brooding letter to Weintraub that vividly captures the mood of those early days in London and the writer's lonely life even at home. And it gives us a glimpse, a snapshot, of Cathy.

> Idling abt impotently on a cold night, feeling damn depressed, sipping Nescafe by the fire, Cathy knitting a petticoat....
>
> The book has slowed down on me. These things happen. I know they happen. But each day you sit vacant writing nothing but still a prisoner to the typewriter—each day like that is a special kind of hell. Questions come to you making small wounds. Why are you making this book? Does it matter? Do you believe in it? That's when you get up and have a cigarette and/or a cup of coffee. Then, a short walk. Then another cigarette ... I thk art or attempts at art are born of despair.

Brian Moore and his wife, Jackie Sirois, visited the couple at their basement flat in Hampstead in March the following year, and there duly followed nights of seemingly endless pub-crawling, which must have been a relief from the nights of doubt and despair. Moore found Mordecai and Cathy's flat dingy but not uncomfortable and, as he wrote back to Weintraub, "admired the fact that he seems able to work anywhere." Richler's living condition made Moore appreciate his own comfortable Montreal setup, though of course he was ten years older. He had yet to publish his first serious novel, but meanwhile he wrote pulp thrillers, some under rather colourful pseudonyms. He observed, somewhat critically, that Mordecai was too concerned with money—which was natural, since the man was broke, dependent on his partner, and determined to become self-sufficient on his writing. And, he said, Mordecai had picked up a slight British Caribbean accent. If he had, it did not last.

The Acrobats was published in the spring of 1954, but not before Richler agreed to a few changes to satisfy the printers, who had refused to go ahead on the grounds that its language was obscene or blasphemous in places. Richler, for example, agreed to change "tits" to "breasts," "kick you in the balls" to "kick you where it hurts," and "bloody christ" to "christ." The book received mixed reviews. A fair smattering of London's literati attended the launch party at Athill's, including Louis MacNeice, the poet. The young author was thrilled to no end. There were people present who actually knew T.S. Eliot as "Tom" and William Faulkner as "Bill"! Soon afterwards, Richler went to Germany to promote the book and also visited France, where he met up with old friends. This time he did not like Paris, found it full of pretentious people. "Honest, Paris is shit ... American one-year crap artists ... Paris Review and Merlin crowd. Everyone an editor and writer and conforming non-conformist." Hadn't he been one of them, only a few years before? Exactly. Which was why he saw through them, through all the talk. He had moved on. Weintraub, never to balk as a gentle scold, took his friend to task for his quick judgment of the city they had loved.

There is no doubt some posturing involved in this attitude, a little showboating, natural in a first-time young novelist. He now belongs in the company of a select few. After a long and uncertain apprenticeship, he has been admitted to the literary pantheon, among the great and the glamorous. Perhaps, he thinks, a more critical acumen and distanced attitude are expected from him, as someone who has created complex characters struggling with complex and universal issues. The truth of course is that the next book awaits to be accomplished, writing which means to return daily to the loneliness of the work desk, stare at the raw page on the typewriter, and resurrect all those doubts of before; the new one will be judged harshly; and that first one, perhaps, doesn't seem so great after all.

How good is *The Acrobats*? It is a young man's book and somewhat derivative. Friends and critics saw in it echoes of Hemingway, Sartre, and Malraux. But it had a good share of very positive reviews, which must have warmed the author's heart. Even he knew its limitations as a first book. For a person of twenty-two, it is a remarkable achievement nonetheless. Richler himself, later, didn't think much of it and kept it out of print; it was reissued only after his death. His editor at Deutsch, writing many years later, wondered, "What on earth made us take it on? It really is very bad." This may be too harsh and defensive in retrospect, but she had by this time published the best of Naipaul, Roth, Mailer, and indeed Richler. It was not the book they had acquired as much as its writer, his potential and dedication, and Athill, answering her own question, commends herself and Andre Deutsch for having recognized this. It is the kind of break a beginning writer needs; Richler was lucky to receive it, but he had worked hard and believed in himself to an extraordinary degree.

That August, in London, Mordecai and Cathy got married. It was she who brought the subject up, and he said, "I don't really want to get married, but I don't want to lose you either." That is what Cathy would remember. It was not exactly holding a gun to his head. She had supported him for a year; no doubt she had also cooked for him and done his laundry. Richler would later say he agreed because he felt compassion for her. And perhaps guilt. It is Florence who puts the finger on the situation: "Most of us are lonely, and most of the mistakes we make in any relationship are because of loneliness." How true. Richler needed Cathy to be by his side on cold, lonely London nights, forget the food and the laundry.

After the wedding ceremony his agent Joyce Weiner gave a luncheon in celebration. Among the guests were a young George Lamming, Brian Moore, and E.M. Forster. Lamming, from the West Indies, had already published (1953) his groundbreaking semi-autobiographical novel, *In the Castle of My Skin*. Mordecai Richler was finishing his own autobiographical novel, *Son of a Smaller Hero*. He gave a big celebration party for his wedding, during which William Weintraub made a congratulatory trunk call from Montreal, which was the talk of the town, so rare and expensive were these long-distance calls.

In 1955 Cathy had a miscarriage; Richler was not unhappy. One wonders how Cathy felt. One recalls Helen.

MORDECAI AND CATHY'S CIVIL MARRIAGE was not only a question of how much love the couple shared, which was what their London friends might have asked. It was something that devastated the family back home, for it went against the tribe.

When news of the proposed nuptial with a shiksa (gentile) reached Montreal, Mordecai's older brother Avrum sent off a long letter in an attempt to dissuade him. The letter is remarkable, first, because it reflects an attitude to assimilation and intermarriage that for Jews in North America today is no longer so prevalent. And second, it is written, mostly, with Lily in mind. "The shock of the news is still around," wrote Avrum, "and it was a shock … because of what it's done to Mom…. She is quite ill over the whole business. It seems that you had given her your word that you wouldn't marry a gentile, much less an older woman."

What lies behind this letter, to which there is more, is anybody's guess. Did Lily put Avrum up to it? Did Avrum use Lily's name, knowing Mordecai was close to her? Avrum concluded his letter with a plea for tribal loyalty: "Think it over many times … think of your ancestors, & of your descendants.... It can't do you or your name, or your career, any earthly good."

And Moe's response? Moe, who so rarely chided Mordecai, who collected clippings and magazines and sent them to his son, who kept him informed about the family— Clifford got his diploma, Cousin Mike sneezed then fainted. He had already in the past expressed his concerns about Mordecai's possible "religious deviations," to which Mordecai had replied that the suspicions were "absolutely silly!" The old man was furious, Avrum now wrote to his brother, punctuating with two exclamation marks. And the old man was. He wrote, on July 24, 1954:

> Dear Son;—
>
> ... Now you have struck the blow, and where it hurts, not the pocket book this time, but person-ally. You take it for granted that I would be agree-able, and bless this unholy marriage, and seal it with a gift cheque, but I am sorry that I have to disappoint you. You also know that up till now I always did your bidding without hesitation, with money, with parcels, and also I had to defend your character.... I was beginning to be proud of you when your first book came out, and was able to have more confidence in you, that some day soon,

perhaps you'll come out with a good book, and being successful, you would find yourself a proper lifemate....

For Moe, success meant financial, and a good book was one that made money. He had the impression that Cathy was a European, used to chocolates and nylons from expatriate North Americans, who had now latched on to Mordecai as a rich Canadian who could give her a better life. He goes on, in perhaps the longest letter he wrote to his son. He could be a soft touch with money, but now

> ... I have to be stern and very hard when it comes to honour, and respect. You will dishonour me when you go through with your plans, and I see no alternative but to do what I see fit. You will have to forget my address, and not try to see me, because seeing you after then will only reopen the wounds of sorrow....

It is up to Mordecai to choose between "an unwelcome woman" and his father, who wishes him to be happy "with respect from the family, and respect from your people, your birthright."

The letter seems to have caught Richler by surprise. He found it somewhat funny, he wrote to Weintraub, but also very human. The fact that he confided in his friend suggests that nevertheless he was disturbed by it. What response he had expected from his family is not clear. But in his reply to his father he takes a high tone and states his beliefs as he has developed them. This is a far cry from the boy in Ibiza begging his father not to abandon him, or the young author wondering what was wrong with assimilation. He wrote now:

> The Jewish tradition is not dependent on what kind of meat you eat or what God the woman you love was brought up to believe in.... I am—like it or not—more within the truly Jewish tradition than any of the Richlers. I know more abt it, am better educated to it, and am more sensitive to its implications. Yr father worshiped God the way other ignorant men long before him worshiped stones....

He goes on to call his grandfather, Shmariyahu Richler, a petty thief. "You are, fundamentally," he says to Moe, "a much more decent person." And, "my attachment to you is stronger, and I hope you'll reconsider yr harshness."

He also can't resist adding that he will bring honour to the family and lists his accomplishments so far. However far he moves away from them in his attitudes, he seems to be saying, he is still a part of them. His glory is theirs. And we cannot help thinking, he is still young.

It is unclear how and to what degree Moe carried out his threat, what he could actually do. One imagines his predicament, having gone through a humiliating marriage himself, now facing the community every day and defending a son who had written a book of dubious merit and got married to a shiksa. There appear to be no letters from him until several years later. Then, Cathy is referred to as "your wife," never by name. Mordecai Richler, in his moving tribute to his father upon his death, chose to remain silent about his rejection of Cathy.

Lily, on the other hand, as early as 1955 and despite what Avrum wrote to Mordecai about her reaction to news of the marriage, could write (in one of the very few letters available from that time): "Give my love to Cathy. Loads and loads of love. Mother." She was not one to let go, but then she was the insecure one.

HE WAS DOING anything he could to raise money—writing the odd magazine article, selling a story to the CBC or to some periodical, applying to the Canada Council. He even thought of applying to the Canadian Jewish Congress for a $1,000 grant, in return for acknowledging it in all editions of his next book. He gave that up. It was not a good idea, anyway, considering the offence that book would cause. Foreign rights to *The Acrobats* were gradually selling, though advances were meagre and royalties were not due for months, if at all. He was excited about Simone de Beauvoir reading his novel for *Les Temps Modernes,* news given to him by Ellen Wright, Richard Wright's wife; nothing came of it. His father, before the breakup, sent food parcels, including precious cigarettes. William Weintraub faithfully sent magazines from Canada. Richler read American novels for his publisher, for modest pay. He attempted writing (or having Cathy write) pornography, for quick money. With Brian Moore he discussed collaborating on a crime thriller; that didn't pan out either.

A typical scene in the Richler household on Winchester Road is described by Weintraub, who visited London in 1956, to Moore: "a real lit factory with George Lamming batting out a novel in guest room, Mort polishing novel in front room, and Cathy doing script-typing for Reuben Ship in kitchen."

In 1954, the year of the British publication of *The Acrobats,* Richler completed a draft of his second novel, called "Losers" and eventually to be published as *Son of a Smaller Hero.* In a letter to Weintraub, describing the novel, Richler said it would trace the development of Jewish life in the Montreal ghetto. He expected to be criticized. "The only people who would consider this bk anti-Semitic ... are those Jews who are very frightened. I don't consider myself a Jewish or a Canadian writer. I am a writer. I'm not interested in the fact that Jews can't get into certain hotels or golf courses. I'm interested in Jews as individual persons...." And, perhaps alarmingly for some, "Briefly, you can put it this way: I think those who were murdered at Dachau should not be mourned as Jews but as men."

Evidently he's still struggling with issues of identity and assimilation, as he had done in Ibiza when preparing "The Rotten People," which also is a very personal book. In any case, the conclusions of this twenty-three-year-old about the Jews can hardly be taken as written in stone or without inner contradictions. This much was clear: he didn't want to be corralled into a literary ghetto; he didn't want to be a spokesman for a people or a country. He simply wanted to write from what he knew. It was not, it is never, an easy place to be.

The hero, Noah, of *Son of a Smaller Hero* shares his last name, Adler, with Kerman of the "The Rotten People." Both protagonists borrow liberally from the life of their author, and it appears that "The Rotten People" was in fact the progenitor of both *The Acrobats* and *Son of a Smaller Hero*. The latter, though, is set entirely in Montreal, just as the former is set in Spain.

Noah Adler's dictatorial grandfather, his uncles, his unsuccessful father, and strong-willed mother, all are based on Richler's own extended family. To Noah, this Orthodox setup is a cage, with all its psychic comforts and safety, to which he can no longer belong. He leaves eventually for Europe, but not before discovering that he is still a part of them: "I am going and I am not going," he tells his *zeyda*. "I can no more leave you, my mother, or my father's memory than I can renounce myself. But I can refuse to take part in this." In demonstrating an understanding of their hurts, the younger Richler is in fact much kinder to Noah's *zeyda* and mother than he is to their real-life counterparts in the essays he wrote much later in which he described his boyhood, and in his later novels. Although considered an early and therefore not quite mature work, in it the streets of the ghetto come alive, its characters are observed intimately, their voices ring true. It is obvious that here Richler has found his true material, a fictional space he can develop and call his own. One can only imagine his excitement.

His fears about its reception seem surprising today, but he was right, it did cause offence. *Maclean's* awarded the novel first prize in a competition, but its editors refused to serialize it—as the award stipulated—calling the book anti-Semitic. Malcolm Cowley, reader for Viking in England, rejected the novel, saying, "it might well become an anti-Semitic document." Walter Allen for Deutsch, however, said that in it "the Canadian novel emerges for the first time." Obviously, no one could mistake the Main for anywhere else, and Montreal's Jews were living a modern Canadian reality. The book was published by Deutsch in England and distributed in Canada; it had trouble finding a publisher in the United States.

William Weintraub, who had seen the galleys, wrote a seven-page letter expressing disappointment and pointing out numerous errors, instances of bad taste, clichés, and caricatures of Jews. Weintraub warned his friend that he would be accused of anti-Semitism. "But if he [the protagonist, Noah] dislikes Jews I, personally, have trouble feeling sympathy for him. Especially in view of the fact that the Jews he dislikes seem to me to be set up as caricatures and even burlesques.... The rabbi (p. 171) who dips 'his beak' into his black prayer book belongs in an anti-semitic pamphlet. It's hackneyed, in awful taste and very ugly. And there are other offensive burlesques." A damning critique, and Weintraub agonized about having written it, questioned his own motives. But his perceptions echoed those of others.

The novel was published in 1957. The Jewish press condemned it. The *Congress Bulletin* of the Canadian Jewish Congress placed it in the "genre of self-hate," adding that it was "a caricature of Jewish life one might expect in *Der Sturmer* [a Nazi newspaper]." A Jewish reviewer in the *Montreal Star* wrote that the book "should have been clothed in shiny paper and sold under the counter at the corner newsstand."

All these reactions, including Weintraub's, seem gross overstatements by today's standards, though the offence taken by the Richler family is understandable. Richler had done what young writers often do, and not many readers appreciate that a character in a novel, even when directly inspired by a real person, has been shaped by narrative and form, is no longer real. In the larger world, however, Richler had scored. The dreaded second book was out of the way, and critics were awaiting the big success that was surely to come. No one had created Montreal, or any Canadian city, with this same immediacy.

His mother, Lily, had meanwhile obtained a copy from Weintraub and read it. She praised the book, including the portrayal of the Jews and of the ghetto; obviously she saw herself in the character of the mother, and she defended herself.

RICHLER'S FRIENDSHIPS in the 1950s reflected his attraction to liberal-left politics. His own background was working class, from Montreal's Jewish ghetto, with its cold-water flats and their outside staircases—where his neighbours included peddlers, plumbers, tailors, factory workers, and taxi drivers. At Sir George Williams College, run by the YMCA, the student body was for the most part left-leaning and activist, and during Richler's time there it had agitated against anti-Semitism and for allowing communists to speak on campus.

Fifties London was home to many young people from the colonies of Africa and the Caribbean. West Indian writer George Lamming would come around to the Richler house; the two would frequent the Mandrake Club, a haunt for the artistic types, which Brian Moore, visiting Richler in 1954, had described—with a touch of envy, perhaps—as "a club with bearded Britishers, black Little Englanders, all sorts of … phony lit people." Doris Lessing, recently from Rhodesia (now Zimbabwe), was also a good friend. Her place was frequented by some of Africa's future leaders, currently agitating for the independence of their countries. Richler mentions them only in passing. There was a prolonged and brutal guerrilla war in Malaya and another one in Kenya, which quite gripped the Western world—many still recall them—but in his letters from those times, his novels, and his recollections,

Richler (with perhaps one minor instance) is silent about them. One concludes that this other world, so much also a part of London, capital of a now-defunct empire, and close to his friends Lamming and Lessing, was alien to him. Lessing, in her autobiography, certainly spends a long time on this involvement in her life. And while Richler had delighted in meeting the older and established E.M. Forster and Archibald MacLeish, British writers closer to his age, including "The Angry Young Men"—Kingsley Amis, John Osborne, and others—who defined the literature of the time in their country, were not part of his circle.

His closest buddies in London, starting in the mid-1950s, were in fact fellow Canadian and American expatriates, mostly Jews, from film and TV, who had been blacklisted for their politics. They included television and film writers Ted Allan, Reuben Ship, and Stanley Mann, all former Montrealers. London was attractive to the Canadians because it had a booming television industry, and they could work without permits. Allan, an ardent communist since his youth, had co-authored a bestselling biography of Norman Bethune, with whom he had served in the Spanish Civil War. Ship, named as a communist for his left-wing activities, had been declared an enemy alien in the United States and was deported to Canada in 1953 in handcuffs and on crutches; he subsequently wrote a much-celebrated radio satire on McCarthyism, *The Investigator* (1954), that was broadcast on CBC and went on to become an underground classic. Mann's credits would include the screenplay for the film adaptation of John Fowles's *The Collector* (1965). In 1957 this expatriate group was joined by Ted Kotcheff, a director from Toronto who had worked at CBC. It is remarkable what a vital role that organization played in nurturing creative film and writing talent at the time.

RICHLER HAD SET his recent novel in the Montreal of his younger days. What better subject next than to examine the lives of himself and his acquaintances as left-wing exiles in London? In the novel that he published next, called *A Choice of Enemies,* he does exactly that. It would seem that two tendencies were competing within him—to bring to life Montreal's ghetto or to be the cosmopolitan commentator on life's great questions, through the medium of fiction. Of course, the former does not preclude the latter. But it runs the risk of becoming marginalized. As the *TLS* reviewer of *Son* wrote, "Jewish writers are always in danger of becoming fascinated by the problems of Jewry to exclusion of all other interests, so that Mr Richler's next novel will be awaited with anxiety as well as hope...." One wonders what other interests the reviewer had in mind. The problems of the English middle classes? Why couldn't "the problems of Jewry," looking beyond differences, be also the problems of others?

A Choice of Enemies describes the 1950s expatriate London of Mordecai Richler, a city to which colonials still flocked from the vestiges of the far-flung Empire, drab and grey, often miserable, always lonely. Many of them would stay and progress and transform themselves, becoming British of sorts, acquiring accents and manners—or, more exactly, finishing them, for British ways were not alien to them. Their children and grandchildren would go on to become part of a new and arguably much more exciting multicultural Britain. Richler and his friends, a generation or a little more removed from their Eastern European Jewish ancestry, were North Americans formed in the cauldrons of the immigrant neighbourhoods of the great cities to which their grandfathers had arrived to start new lives. They did not share a culture with England. (It is interesting to note that Indians have had greater contact with Britain.) These North Americans, as fictionalized in *A Choice of Enemies,* form a foreigners' clique, with no intention of integrating, and little empathy for the host society.

> Proud they were. They had come to conquer.
> Instead they were being picked off one by one by

the cold, drink, and indifference. They abjured taking part in the communal life. They mocked the local customs from the school tie to queuing, and were for the most part free of them by dint of their square, classless accents. Unlike their forebears, they were punk imperialists. They didn't marry and settle down among the natives. They had brought their own women and electric shavers with them.... For even those who had lived in London for years only knew the true life of the city only as a rumour. Around and around them the natives, it seemed, were stirred by Diana Dors, a rise in bus fares, test matches, automation, and Princess Margaret. The aliens knew only other aliens.

In this London, the émigrés of *A Choice of Enemies* conform to their own pecking order, as they build up their precarious film and writing careers and work at their fragile social lives. It is this little clique, held together by Canada-America, their fashionably leftist views, their escape from the States worn like a badge of honour, that Mordecai Richler takes apart. Is the choice of good and evil, a choice of sides, a choice of enemies, still possible today as it had been in the recent past—during the Spanish Civil War and the Second World War?

Their certainties begin to unravel when into their little group arrives Ernst, a tall, blond, and very physical and uncouth German. His mere existence among them tests the presumptions of their beliefs. This mysterious German must likely have escaped something; he must have been a Nazi, a Hitler Youth. They hate him, abuse him, but lack that legitimizing certainty. The exception is Norman Price, a principled and gifted but somewhat weak man. That he is a WASP may not lack significance, for Richler often portrays the WASP as weak. When Norman refuses to judge Ernst, in fact tries to help him, he is subjected, with great irony, to the sort of inquisition that the exiles have escaped from, in the United States.

But Norman does not come out of this with any moral certainty or victory; he too is taken apart. For as a survivor in postwar Europe, Ernst has lived the life of a petty criminal and has recently killed by accident a young soldier who happens to have been Norman's beloved younger brother Nick. This incident inserted at the beginning holds the novel's tension, because Norman does not know of Ernst's deed, and we await to discover how he will respond when the time comes. To add to Norman's angst, a young Canadian innocent with whom Norman is in love turns out to have fallen for Ernst. The plot is clever.

The novel on the one hand examines meaning in the lives of the postwar generation, questioning the certainties of good and evil; it is also very Canadian: Montreal and Toronto lurk in the background as permanent presences, and the wishy-washy but decent Norman represents the more genteel face of the old Canada. In contrast to his ilk, *A Choice of Enemies* highlights the generation of postwar Jews, no longer the frightened inhabitants of the shtetls but strong, aggressive, and successful. They represent a new Canada. And Mordecai Richler, one of them, was already being celebrated back home for having injected a new sort of excitement into Canadian letters.

IN THE SUMMER OF 1958, Mordecai Richler and his wife Cathy stayed with Stanley and Florence Mann in a rented villa in Roquebrune, by the sea, near Monte Carlo. One afternoon when Cathy returned from the beach, Mordecai told her he no longer loved her, their marriage was over; he was in love with Florence. Stanley had gone to London at the time.

Mordecai and Florence's is a rare love story, a romantic tale of two people ideally suited and lucky enough to find each other and spend their lives together. It defined Richler's life thereafter, as a writer who was a devoted family man; it inspired the subplots and settings of several novels; and it defined Florence as Mrs. Richler, his companion and support, his anchor. Arguably she was the hero of his life story. Cathy is cast in the role of the loser, but this is partly because we know so little of her.

Florence Mann was "drop-dead" gorgeous, according to those who knew her. She was a successful model in London at the time, and a favourite story told about her is that she had been pursued by both Sean Connery and Christopher Plummer. Her marriage to Stanley Mann, the film writer, was not working out; by many accounts he was a philanderer. In 1957 they had separated, and taking the villa in France that summer in 1958 was an attempt to get back together. Her maiden name was Florence Wood; she had been adopted by a couple named Ethel and Albert Wood soon after her birth, in 1929, and brought up in the Montreal working-class neighbourhood of Pointe-Saint-Charles. Finding out about the adoption in her teenage years was a traumatic experience, more so because she could not subsequently discover the identities of her birth parents, the records having been destroyed in a fire. This disappointment had left her with an unhappy sense of incompleteness. She married Stanley Mann in 1953, having met him while working as a model and actress in Montreal. This was the year Mordecai was in Montreal, but she did not see him.

As she tells the story in an interview, one day Ted Allan gave her the manuscript of Mordecai's first novel, *The Acrobats,* to read, which the author had left with him. She was impressed by it, as she reported to Allan, coming as it did from such a young man.

The Manns and the Allans were friends. Ted and Kate Allan went to London, where prospects seemed bright in film and television; Stanley and Florence Mann followed. It was at the Allans' house that Florence and Mordecai first met briefly. She would recall a strange and very awkward young man, yet appealing and sensitive. He had a powerful effect on her. It was the day before his marriage to Cathy. The following day, at his wedding reception, Richler offered to get Florence a drink and followed her to the bar, very obviously smitten. Over the months his friends gradually came to know of his attraction to Florence. They warned him against being silly. Recollections of this growing romance decades later undoubtedly bear the character of legend, part of Richler lore. Richler himself fictionalized the story in his final novel, *Barney's Version.* Did Richler, then, live a lie with Cathy? Perhaps only partly. And Cathy? Years later Brian Moore wrote with relish to Weintraub that Kotcheff had told him that Cathy had been "tromping" Richler, that is, was unfaithful to him. The truth of the statement is anybody's guess; there is no other indication of it.

By 1957 Florence's marriage was already on the rocks; there was a child by then, called Daniel. And Mordecai, who with Cathy would visit the Manns for an occasional drink, meet them at expatriate parties, and was a friend of Stanley's, became more and more obsessed with Florence. Once, as she recalls, he came to visit her in her apartment. She and Stanley had separated; Daniel, who was a few months old, was with her. She and Mordecai went out for a walk, and there he told her he found it difficult to be just near her; he was in love with her and had been for some time. She was surprised, not offended. He kissed her on the cheek and departed. Subsequently she described him to her analyst as a difficult personality who had problems with people, but added, "Of all the people I have met in the past few years, he is perhaps the only one whose intelligence I admire and respect and is a man I would trust completely." She had found the right man.

Cathy was bitter and angry. "I had looked after him, made his meals, entertained his friends," she would say later. But they had had good times together, partying until 4 A.M., making latkes, travelling. Following that unhappy afternoon when Richler gave her the news, Cathy moved to

Villefranche, a fishing village nearby, where she gave swimming lessons at an American children's camp. Mordecai was left in the villa with Florence, and Ted Kotcheff, who had come to visit.

Florence and Ted soon left, and Mordecai stayed behind by himself to finish his fourth novel, *The Apprenticeship of Duddy Kravitz,* which he would dedicate to her. On July 25, from France, he wrote a dejected letter to William Weintraub, giving him news of the breakup.

The irony in all this was that Florence always liked Cathy and understood her. Cathy had a nervous breakdown at some point and later apparently became a Buddhist nun. Richler would continue to support her for a few years.

BY THIS TIME, in 1958, Mordecai Richler's financial prospects were at last beginning to look brighter.

Only a year before, in June 1957, Richler had written to Weintraub from Tourrettes-sur-Loup, his former haunt on the Riviera where he had first come from Spain; he was holidaying with Cathy and there was no hint of the marital problem. Financially he was not doing very well, and he wrote that it was 90 percent certain that the two of them would be returning to Canada. He hoped that he would find a film job, and he might need to borrow $500 from his friend. He planned to stay in Toronto, not Montreal, perhaps to avoid problems with his father. It appears that Richler did go to Canada briefly by himself at the end of that year, but there was no job, and he returned to London. This was for the best, judging by the turn his personal life and his career were about to take.

A few months after his return, early in 1958 he received a grant from the newly formed Canada Council to work on the manuscript of his new novel. And then the breakup with Cathy in July, back in France.

It was with television and film writing that the avenue to financial security finally opened up to him. He had already written some material for the CBC. In London, his Canadian friends in the business had found him commissions, mostly hack writing, good to make a living while he wrote his fiction, and sometimes he would use a pseudonym for this purpose. He seemed to possess a knack for the work. With Ted Allan he had co-authored scripts for a Robin Hood serial, using the very Anglo-Saxon name of John Snow. Ship had sent him some work, which included an early Peter Sellers comedy.

Now Ted Kotcheff was working for the Sunday-night program for ABC-TV called *Armchair Theatre,* which brought socially relevant drama to a large British public. Its producer was Sydney Newman, also from Canada and the CBC. Kotcheff had already read and liked *The Acrobats,* on the basis of which he had met Richler at Tourrettes-sur-Loup in the summer of '57, when, famously, Richler had hardly spoken a word. But Richler had subsequently written a letter of apology, saying he had been too absorbed with his novel during their meeting, and the two made up and went on to become the closest of friends and collaborators. Kotcheff's first directorial assignment in London was the production of an old British drama called *The Sunshine Hour* for television. The normal fee for such an assignment was £15, but the script on hand was so bad that Kotcheff got Richler to write a new one, for £100. This was a fortune. Over the 1958–59 seasons, Mordecai Richler and Ted Kotcheff went on to make four other collaborations for *Armchair Theatre.* Currently not listed among its best offerings, they nevertheless at the time brought Richler much-needed financial relief.

Greater lucre was in the movies. An English producer named Jack Clayton happened to be making his first feature film in 1958, called *A Room at the Top,* based on a novel by John Braine. The existing film script was deemed not satisfactory, and Mordecai Richler was hired to do the doctoring. He was paid £500 but, by prior agreement, was not credited. The film went on to win a British film award and two

Academy Awards, for best actress (Simone Signoret) and for best adapted screenplay (Neil Patterson). Following this success, Richler began to be called upon regularly as a screenwriter. He would work for a few weeks, make a small "fortune," and get on with his real passion. As he wrote to Weintraub: "am very financially solid, embarrassingly so, and I can dilly dally with my novel for months and months, which was the general idea.... If things break as well as they indicate, next year I will give a grant to the Canada Council." He did start sending money to his still struggling father. Fifty dollars on Father's Day.

The success of *A Room at the Top* turned Jack Clayton, also nominated for the Academy Award for best direction, into an internationally renowned filmmaker who specialized in turning literary genres into movies. Coincidentally, his last feature film was based on a book by a former Montrealer and a friend of Richler's, Brian Moore.

CHAPTER FIVE

Duddy Kravitz and Away

Fortune favoured the brave. Richler had taken a bold, some might even say brash, first step by going away, young, inexperienced, and without any money of his own, to become a writer. He had struggled to survive, begged and borrowed, and he surely suffered private agonies about which he remained silent. But he was also lucky in having received an early break at being published, making devoted friends despite his reserve and "strangeness," and acquiring some measure of financial security through writing television and film scripts. He became a respected writer, though the first three novels had not sold well and received mixed reviews. In 1958 he finished *The Apprenticeship of Duddy Kravitz,* which was published the following year. It met with immediate enthusiasm on both sides of the Atlantic, and he emerged at last into the limelight as a major writer.

THE APPRENTICESHIP OF DUDDY KRAVITZ is a novel about a conniving young product of Montreal's Jewish ghetto as he struggles and schemes to push himself out of working-class poverty. Duddy is the younger of the two sons of widowed taxi driver Max. There is, as we meet him at age fifteen, nothing likeable about him. While his brother Lennie is away becoming a doctor like a good Jewish boy, Duddy leads a hyperactive gang of mischief-makers in the school and on the streets. His pranks are relentless and merciless, and it turns out he may even have driven the Scottish teacher Mr. MacPherson's wife to her death by one of his obscene phone calls. He is uncouth and vulgar, without a hint of a conscience. But even in the early stages of this book, as we see him characterized and presented thus, we already wonder, Is his manner so surprising? For, as the author informs us, "Where Duddy Kravitz sprung from the boys grew up dirty and sad, spiky also, like grass beside the railway tracks. He might have been born in Lodz, but forty-eight years earlier his grandfather had bought a steerage passage to Halifax."

Needless to say this is Richler's own dear Montreal, the Jewish area around the Main reproduced with intimacy and close attention to detail.

> To a middle-class stranger, it's true, one street would have seemed as squalid as the next. On each corner a cigar store, a grocery, and a fruit man. Outside staircases everywhere. Winding ones,

wooden ones, rusty and risky ones. Here a prized plot of grass splendidly barbered, there a spitefully weedy patch. An endless repetition of precious peeling balconies and waste lots making the occasional gap here and there. But, as the boys knew, each street between St Dominique and Park Avenue represented subtle differences in income. No two cold-water flats were alike.

The streets are identifiable, the characters sound familiar; and Fletcher's Field High School is but a thinly fictionalized version of the famous Baron Byng High School on St. Urbain Street. It is *the* Jewish high school but, as Mr. MacPherson knows, will not be so for long because his students are moving up, and their children will not attend here. This novel is how Duddy Kravitz, hardly the school's pride, escapes the ghetto.

There is an abiding sadness to Duddy Kravitz, whom even his father, Max, calls "a dope like me"; who grows up on Max's fanciful heroic stories of the Jewish Boy Wonder only to discover that he was no hero at all, just a petty criminal. Duddy's life begins its transformation when, having graduated four hundred and tenth from Fletcher's Field, he goes to work as a waiter during the summer season at Rubin's Hotel Lac des Sables in the resort area of Sainte-Agathe-des-Monts in the Laurentians. Among the seasonal waiters he is the only one not from college, the only one from a humble background; an uncouth outsider whose language gives him away as one from the ghetto, he is taunted and despised. But one quality Duddy Kravitz possesses: he does not allow himself to be crushed. One day, while out on a jaunt with French-Canadian hotel maid Yvette, he discovers an isolated lake in the woods, and in the firm belief impressed upon him by his *zeyda* that a man is nothing without land, he resolves to acquire all the real estate around the lake. This becomes his obsession; it will be his lifeline. There is nothing he will not do to acquire the separate subdivisions of the land. He lies, he cheats, he makes artistic mockery of middle-class bar mitzvah ceremonies, which he undertakes to film with no experience of his own and the help of a drunken English director. His use of his girlfriend, Yvette, and his epileptic American assistant Virgil, is callous. And yet one roots for him. This is the only way he can win, big or small. Not with looks, small and scrawny as he is and struggling to grow a beard; not with influence or birthright; not with conventional brains. But by being a *pusherke,* a scheming go-getter, "a little Jew-boy on the make," as his Uncle Benjy calls him. He may not have academic smarts, but he has street smarts. He wins grudging admiration for his successes but no sympathy for his setbacks. Nobody roots for him. And at the end, when he wins, we wonder, Did he really win? He's lost Yvette and Virgil; his brother Lennie and father, Max, are not impressed; and his *zeyda* walks away from him because of the way he has acquired the land. But the barman calls him Mr. Kravitz and opens a tab in his name.

ALTHOUGH RICHLER had introduced the vernacular of St. Urbain previously, *Duddy Kravitz* is the novel in which it finds its full glory. The ghetto is given to us in its own language—the easy informality, the casual vulgarity, the Yiddish inflection, and above all the inventiveness and humour of an essentially oral culture. "Do you all know what a penis is?" asks the enlightened Mrs. Cox, attempting to do something about the boys' language. "Sure," Duddy says. "A penis is a guy that plays the piano." And here's Max, holding forth at Eddy's Cigar & Soda, next to the taxi stand, telling his favourite story about the Jewish Boy Wonder to a bunch of wisecracks who've heard it a dozen times before.

> Max waited. He sucked a sugar cube. "Anyway, he's broke, like I said. So he walks up to the corner of Park and St Joseph and hangs around

the streetcar stop for a couple of hours, and do you know what?"

"He trips over a hundred dollar bill and breaks his leg."

"He's pulled in for milking pay phones. Or stealing milk bottles, maybe."

"All that time," Max said, "he's collecting streetcar transfers off the street and selling them, see. Nerve? *Nerve....*"

While *Son of a Smaller Hero* is an inward-looking, introspective drama, its tensions derived mainly from the conditions within an extended family and Noah's desire to escape it, *Duddy Kravitz* takes in a larger slice of Montreal. Artistically, it is the flowering of the world first introduced in the earlier novel. And while the themes of the novel are far from trivial, its native humour frees it from the trap of sincerity.

The novel has been said, like other "Jewish novels," to depict the assimilation of the Jew into America or Canada. Such a formulaic sociological reading, alas a too-easy teaching tool, denies the particularity of the novel, its setting and its characters, let alone the quality of its writing and inventiveness. If there is such a thing as a mainstream, its granularity has to be acknowledged. It is not so easy to define anymore. Today, Margaret Laurence, or indeed even Margaret Atwood, is as ethnic as Richler or Rohinton Mistry. Moreover, in this day when cultural diversity is celebrated in a globalized world—and even in the melting pot, what does one assimilate to?—Richler's book has resonance for Jews across many borders, as it has for non-Jews in different ways. By the same token, the readership of Canadian novels spans the world. *The Apprenticeship of Duddy Kravitz* is, therefore, first and foremost a novel about a *pusherke* who happens to be a Jew in Montreal.

When the novel came out, many Jews were shocked that such an unlikeable fellow, an unethical, grasping young man, was depicted as one of them. Close-contained communities naturally get nervous at seeing their laundry hung out for the world to see; a novel does that in unexpected and shocking ways. *Duddy Kravitz* seemed to be playing up to anti-Semitic stereotypes. As a character in the novel, the son of a wealthy Jewish family, says, "It's the cretinous little money-grubbers like Kravitz that cause antisemitism." Anti-Semitism indeed is present throughout the novel; but it is not the author who is anti-Semitic. We see its awareness in the characters, and we see it portrayed in incidents, as when a teacher asks the boys, as a joke, how the Jews make an S, and illustrates his answer by drawing the dollar sign on the board. The author ameliorates the unpleasantness of anti-Semitism with humour, makes it less uncomfortable, just as the blacks in North America have used humour to soften the pain and memories of racism. With time, however, Jewish insecurities about *Duddy Kravitz* have largely abated. The rest of us feel fortunate that people among us whom we might have seen as alien are shown to be just like us. That is the power and gift of literature. The novel is now a Canadian classic, Duddy Kravitz a proverbial figure. There are Duddy Kravitzes wherever there are little boys trying to break out from poverty in a world loaded against them. In 1975 Ted Kotcheff made a highly successful film of *Duddy Kravitz,* with the screenplay written by Richler himself.

There is some truth to Brian Moore's observation that the non-Jewish characters in this book are all flat. In particular, Yvette could have been conceived in greater depth. We don't know much about her, she comes and goes, though it could be argued that her world and Duddy's are far apart, and it is his world that is the novel's concern. Hers is out there somewhere. This is not entirely convincing, for she must come surely bearing the imprint of her world upon her. In fact, throughout Richler's work, the francophones receive rather summary treatment, if at all. There was, by Richler's own accounts, and as reflected in the novels, little social interaction between the Jews of the ghetto and the French Canadians who were their neighbours a few blocks away. The accommodation was toward the WASP and English Canada, which fact Richler acknowledged elsewhere. He also agreed, in a letter to Weintraub, that "Yvette doesn't quite come off. This kind of thg I hope to remedy, too, but I also fear a congenital weakness in the creation of women characters."

Moore's novel *The Lonely Passion of Judith Hearne,* incidentally, after receiving numerous rejections, had been published in 1955 after Richler's recommendation of it to his editor, Diana Athill. The resemblance of this title to *The Apprenticeship of Duddy Kravitz* and *A House for Mr. Biswas,* by V.S. Naipaul, another writer known to Richler and published by the same house, is interesting and perhaps nothing more. Naipaul's book appeared in 1961. The colonial worlds of Duddy Kravitz, Judith Hearne, and Mr. Biswas, however, couldn't have been more different.

AFTER MORDECAI had parted with Cathy at Tourrettes-des-Loup in the summer of 1958, he returned to their Winchester Road flat in London, which he now shared with his friend Ted Kotcheff. This seems to have been one of the happiest periods in his life. Money was good, and the flat, well stocked with Scotch, was a place of lively entertainment. It was a period of friendship and creativity, of supreme confidence for the two of them; they had no doubt they would make it big in their respective careers, as indeed they did. In a letter to Weintraub dated November 8 of that year, Richler wrote with exuberance:

> Am really beat, man ... Abt the work, man, I wrote [finished *Duddy Kravitz*] a novel, rewrote a film, adapted a TV play, wrote two original TV plays, several stories, articles, and two radio plays. I AM TIRED. I DESERVE A REST, what?
>
> Am in a waiting and party-going period. Brian tells me you thk I am happy, or I sound happy, or something, and what if I am, man?

He bought a tuxedo to attend a ball.

His friend Kotcheff gives us an idea of the discipline by which Mordecai lived. After making himself a breakfast of salami and eggs or an omelette, he would read two or three papers, then go to his typewriter and start clacking away until twelve. He would get up and walk to Finchley Road and buy a deli sandwich and the *Herald Tribune* (for the sports scores), eat his corned beef sandwich with pickles, and take a nap until two, after which he would be back at his typewriter until five. Then he would make himself a gin and tonic, and the two of them would go out to eat. His former wife, Cathy, confirms this description of Richler's discipline, including the nap between writing spells. That's all he ever wanted to do (i.e., write), she said. When he was married to her, of course, she cooked for him, and he had less money. Explaining his writing habit to a curious Kotcheff, who inquired why he did not wait for the muse to arrive but started clacking away as soon as he had sat down, he said, "Ted, if I sat around waiting for inspiration, I'd never write a bloody word."

He was happiest when he wrote. And now he had Florence. The two of them were waiting for their divorces to come through so they could be married. She was already a top model, had worked for Sassoon and Dior, and during this interim an opportunity came by on the West End for her to act in the stage version of the play *The World of Suzy Wong*. (It would later be made into a well-known movie.) She was given a small part. On her decision would depend the relationship she would have with Mordecai. He of course pretended that he did not mind: she had a whole career in front of her; why give it up? But she knew he did not want her to take the offer; he was possessive. And so she chose not to become an actress or have her own career, in return for the love and life he gave her.

The following year, the fall of 1959, *Duddy Kravitz* was published in Britain, Canada, and the United States. One day Cathy walked in unannounced at the flat when only Ted Kotcheff was in. She went over to the table, on which lay the recently arrived copies of the American edition. She picked one up, saw the dedication to Florence, and had a fit, ripping the book to bits; she picked up the typewriter and threw it out the back window. As Kotcheff tells it, "And I'm shouting, 'Cathy, stop it!' and finally I walloped her one. I hit her so hard with the flat of my hand I knocked her down. And she was sobbing hysterically, 'All those years, all those years ... I worked so he could write. I supported him. And now he dedicated this novel to this bitch.' She was a curious creature. It was awfully painful."

BY THE END OF SUMMER both their divorces had come through. In December, to get away from it all, Mordecai and Florence flew to Holland with three-year-old Daniel, in a small plane that could however also fit their small Renault. They drove to Rome, where they moved into a house, which they were able to rent courtesy of his London publisher. Here Mordecai, in what one can only imagine as a blissfully domesticated life, for the first time with a woman whom he passionately loved, and a child, worked on what he called his

Shalinsky-Griffin novel. Florence was with "issue," he wrote elatedly to Weintraub. They were set to go to Canada. He wrote his plans to Moe, somewhat warily ending with: "Florence is of the Hebrew persuasion by choice ... I naturally expect Daniel—Florence's boy—-to be treated very warmly. I can vouch for his Jewishness having been present at his circumcision." Moe replied, telling him only to be careful on his way back on the snow-covered roads of Europe.

In March 1960, Mordecai, a pregnant Florence, and Daniel left Rome for London, from where they flew to Montreal. They were met by Lily. After staying with Weintraub for a few days, they rented places in both Montreal and Toronto. In August, Florence nine months pregnant, they were married in a Presbyterian church in Montreal. Memories of this wedding too, aided by foggy memories, have attained partly mythic status. Apparently no rabbi would have married the couple. The Christian minister who did so was a woman, who had been warned to make the ceremony short for the sake of the expectant bride and not to get into the Jesus Christ business, but she could not resist a lengthy discourse on the subject of love, and Mordecai was fit to murder her. Two days later the couple and friends went out for a lobster dinner. In the middle of it, Florence's water broke. She was rushed to the hospital and gave birth to a boy, who was named Noah by Ted Kotcheff (who had flown in from London for the wedding), the child's godfather.

Mordecai Richler was now a family man.

CHAPTER SIX

The Writer as
Family Man

The wedding had been a small affair, with a few close friends in attendance; possibly the irrepressible Lily was present too. Members of the Richler clan, as Orthodox Jews, would not have approved his marrying a shiksa. On top of that, not counting that the bride was eminently pregnant, the groom had negatively characterized the family in a book, including its patriarch, and done more of the same to the Jews of Montreal's Main in his recent book, *Duddy Kravitz*. As one of them opined, He drinks, he pisses. None of them, except Mordecai's parents and Uncle Max, came to pay their respects to the couple. Uncle Max brought a present. Moe, when he came, acted very shy with the stunningly beautiful bride from another culture, who looked so different from an Orthodox Jewish woman. "How does she like being a Jew?" he asked his son. She of course had only formally converted, out of convenience, when she married Stanley Mann. When asked to look at the baby, reluctantly Moe followed Florence, Mordecai walking behind them with an amused look. "A baby is a baby," was Moe's simple verdict upon seeing Noah in the cradle. Indeed, just as many others have thought at a similar occasion. But this man of simple tastes and education, who had come from a shtetl in Galicia when he was hardly older than an infant himself, must have wondered, Would the boy be brought up a Jew? It was too much, to be presented not only with a shiksa daughter-in-law but also a grandchild, ready-made, and another one born two days after the wedding. Mordecai had always tested him. He did not believe in the legitimacy of a mixed marriage; he did not think it could work, as he had written before to Mordecai upon his first marriage; he had even sent Mordecai a magazine article explaining why. But then Moe's own marriage had been a disaster, the unhappiness and shame of which had scarred his son.

IN TORONTO AND MONTREAL, the superstar who was a grandson of a major Hasidic rabbi was invited to give talks at synagogues and felt free to vent his opinions on Judaism. His audiences were confused, offended, infuriated. At one question session he was asked why he had not given Duddy Kravitz, hero of his "so-called novel," an Italian name, for instance; and, if on St. Urbain they had called the French Canadians "Frogs," what was the point of telling the world about it?

In a long article he wrote for *Maclean's,* titled "We Jews Are Almost as Bad as the Gentiles," Richler said that after an absence of seven years, he found the changes in the Jewish community "astonishing." Religion had been "modernized and, in the process, emasculated, shorn of most of its beauty and mystery." Where there was one ghetto, now there were several wealthy but similarly exclusive enclaves. Where learned men had commanded respect, now it was those with cash. He goes on thus, in a serious, almost old-fashioned rabbinical vein, but can provide no prescription for being Jewish. Elsewhere he vented on Canadian culture. He gave his views on Canada in an article titled "The White Americans," published in London's *The Spectator.* "Like Jews and homosexuals," he said, "we are quick to claim international celebrities and people of distinction living elsewhere as our very own." Young people left Canada because they got bored with it. "Living in Canada again, as I am right now, one is immediately struck by the fact that there is no indignation here.... Our Canadian society lacks excitement and direction. We are one of the underdeveloped countries.... There's nothing to do here but make more money than your neighbour, and anti-Americanism is reaching such a pitch that I can foresee the day of Castro on our five-dollar bills and an un-Canadian activities committee."

There was a certain arrogance and self-importance in this attitude, but the role of bad boy seemed almost de rigueur under the circumstances. For Mordecai Richler to have made it in England and in the United States gave him a particular status in Canada. A superior attitude toward the limitations of home was also a common colonial affectation of the time; it justified why one had gone away. The haughty V.S. Naipaul, a Trinidadian who was in London and known to Richler, was increasingly called a racist back home for his opinions. At the same time, in the United States, Philip Roth's recent novels had caused both sensation and offence, and Norman Mailer seemed always up to something spectacular. Richler had things to say in Canada, and people paid attention even when he offended. Being blunt was his way, this person of few words of talk, who only said what he meant. One must keep in mind, too, that he was still twenty-nine, one year below the suspect, compromising age of real adulthood.

Still, he was home, and you criticize vehemently only what you care about. To cut yourself off completely you have to stop caring. How could he? The novel which had just propelled him to fame was all about Montreal's Jews, they were a part of him; he was forged in the milieu that was the ghetto, as he liked to call it. He had every right to speak his truth about his people, his country. Having lived away he could as a matter of fact hold them up to objective scrutiny and higher standards. He had his detractors, naturally, but he also had his supporters, for whom he had brought much-needed excitement to the culture debate.

BRIAN MOORE was in Toronto that Christmas and was invited to the Richlers' Boxing Day party, at their rented home at Lawrence and Dufferin. All the literati were there, he reported in a letter to Weintraub: Jack McClelland, Robert Fulford, Robert Weaver, Ross McLean, and Morley Callaghan. Moore reciprocated with dinner at an expensive restaurant where, as he put it, the waiters "warm[ed] the cognac."

> Mort, depressed because it was me who was squandering on the cognac and not him, called for the plug-in telephone and made two long and hideously expensive calls to London, just to say hello. This threw me into a state of nerves, to the extent that I had to have my cognac rewarmed....

"I enjoy these things," said Mort. "You don't know what it's like to once have been poor."

In the late spring of 1961, running short of money, Mordecai and Florence returned to London. Just before they left, Richler learned that he had been awarded a Guggenheim fellowship. On St. Urbain Street, as Moe reported, he and his friends celebrated the award with a cake inscribed with "GUGGENHEIM"; and they nicknamed him "Guggy." Who said the boy didn't belong? Soon after Mordecai's arrival in London, Ted Kotcheff asked him to write the script for a British comedy, *Tiara Tahiti,* starring James Mason and John Mills, "a month's work at an embarrassingly high sum per wk.," as he described the commission to his Canadian publisher Jack McClelland, adding, "I will finally be able to tackle my very own stuff for a long time to come."

He meant his novels, though magazine assignments arrived at his doorstep with a regularity, to tempt and divert him. *Maclean's, Chatelaine, Commentary,* and *Holiday* all beckoned. He went along. The gain was that journalism, to use a broad term for it, would keep him in touch with a reading public and allow him to speak directly. Novelists often feel that in the isolation of their careers, they risk becoming irrelevant storytellers. The world outside is often so much more bizarre and interesting. Surely the writer, as observer, must have something to say about it. People expect it. And the prospect of timely extra cash is not to be scoffed at. But he was walking a tightrope.

Jack McClelland, with whom he had started a growing friendship in Toronto and who would publish him for the next twenty-five years, warned him: "The pay is hardly worth it. I don't think it does one's prestige as a writer any good.... It's an open invitation to other critics and novelists to slander the hell out of your next book when it appears." Here spoke a true literary publisher. During the 1960s, Richler wrote almost thirty journalistic pieces, in addition to film scripts.

By 1963 his enthusiasm regarding his finances had abated, and he was again tempted to take the way of many writers—find a steady job in a related field, such as broadcasting or teaching. He wrote of his decision to a few friends in Canada. He asked McClelland to find him a place to stay in Toronto. And he wrote inquiries about jobs there, but to no avail. Florence, too, was against uprooting the young family. So in England they stayed. They had lived in a small flat in Hampstead; now with three children (Emma was born in 1962), they looked for a bigger place.

Richler asked Brian Moore for a loan toward purchase of a house; Moore generously replied that though he was considering a house himself, he could come up with half the amount, which was the not inconsiderable sum then of $1,500. In 1963 the Richlers found a large house in Surrey. In 1965 a fourth child, Martha, was born, and in 1967 the fifth, Jake. Mordecai Richler, brought up in a broken family, became a family man with a vengeance. And Florence, who had been given away as an infant and never knew her real parents, now had a large brood to call her own. They would be brought up privileged and secular; the boy from Baron Byng enrolled his children in English private schools.

GOING BY THE NAMES of their circle and the people who came to their Surrey house—Sean Connery, Philip Roth, Rod Steiger, Mel Lasky (the editor of *Encounter*), Angus Wilson, Kingsley Amis, Doris Lessing—the Richlers lived a glamorous life. Arguably writers had a greater status in London film circles than in Hollywood. And then there was the Canadian group, a mafia, as someone called it—Ted Kotcheff, Sid Newman, Ted Allan, Reuben Ship, Mordecai Richler, and their wives. They had their beers and Montreal smoked meat, played poker, discussed baseball and hockey. And yet a list of friends and dinner guests is hardly indication of a writer's life. Richler was still a private man, gruff and reserved, single-minded in his needs and pursuits; after marriage he actually withdrew, became engrossed in his family—"disappeared into his marriage," is how his then-editor Diana Athill, who had known Richler for many years in London, puts it. Is it possible that he was happy? Contented, is Mavis Gallant's assessment; deeply contented; but then he was married to Florence. That's too easy, but perhaps a good approximation. Mordecai Richler never revealed himself, except in his writing.

Contented, perhaps, but financial worries still remained. Film scripts were lucrative, journalism brought in extra cash, but these were occasional and piecemeal. There was as yet no big splash with a novel. Mordecai Richler's four novels were not huge sellers, especially in the United States, where it mattered. They were not his main money-makers.

WITH *DUDDY KRAVITZ,* Mordecai Richler knew he had found his true voice, his literary calling. He had in mind now a series of novels about Montreal; in effect, as he put it to Brian Moore in a letter, he desired to be its Balzac or Faulkner. But his stay in Toronto meanwhile had produced a brainwave, an irresistible inspiration for a biting satire on the cultural life of the city, and by extension on the public culture of Canada. The result, published three years later as *The Incomparable Atuk,* is a crisp, fast-paced, and funny novel about the adventures of an Inuit ("Eskimo," then) called Atuk, who is befriended by an RCMP officer on Baffin Bay, introduced to an advertising executive who has flown up north on behalf of a business corporation, and brought to Toronto. Using this "minority" character, a far from noble or simple savage, who is patronized and used politically and culturally but who in turn learns to play the game to his personal advantage, Richler exposes all the pettiness and smallness of the cultural scene as he saw it, hanging out to ridicule the pretensions and absurdities patently obvious in the cultural nationalism of the day, the cynicism and greed of big business, the gullibility of the masses, and the hypocrisies and contradictions of special interest and identity groups. In the process he even foreshadows the more absurd manifestations of the political correctness that was to follow two decades later. Every group is fearlessly caricatured to an extreme—even discomforting—degree: the smelly, simplistic, savage "Eskimo"; the "Negro" stud; the witless WASP; the thin-skinned Jew. In addition, there are characters whose real-life models are easily recognizable to those who were around at the time.

The novel poses issues he would return to again and again. It is a mark of his maturity at this point that he uses the bare bones of a simple, conventional plot on which to pin his criticisms, producing a highly amusing and engaging little novel. His lampoon of the mediocrity lurking behind the mask of nationalism is best demonstrated in the now immortal words "I'm world famous all over Canada," uttered by Dr. Burt Parks, the bodybuilding guru and patriot as he accepts a plaque from the blind bodybuilders of Canada. The requirement for Canadian content on national television, the author tells us, is satisfied by cynically showing such programs early in the morning, for the few desperate souls who watch the tube at this hour. Atuk's argument with Old One about intermarriage could well be that of a young modern Jew, one that indeed Richler himself might have used. It is an argument that any young man from any religious or ethnic background might use. An opinion on Zionism is expressed by Atuk quite innocently when he compares the Eskimos' situation to that of the Palestinians.

The book, however, does raise concerns regarding Richler's attitudes. There is first the arrogance, already mentioned, of a young man who has spent twelve years abroad and returns home briefly to ridicule a country then seeing a real resurgence of cultural and national identity. Richler might answer that he was still very much a Canadian and he called the game as he saw it; not criticizing, playing along with silliness and celebrating mediocrity, would be precisely the attitudes not to take. No one now, forty years later, would argue with that. But it is ironic nonetheless that the provincialism he ridiculed was what in fact gave him the opportunity to express himself. His celebrity, after all, was to a large degree due to his having made it in London and New York.

Did he go too far in his racial caricatures? Richler's fearlessness regarding this aspect of his work was due, one might observe, to the fact that he too came from a people demeaned and put upon for centuries. Racism, caricatures, discrimination? They were his heritage, from the Inquisition and before, through the pogroms and the Holocaust, and the exclusive beaches, clubs, and schools in the Canada of his youth. This gave him licence. He was not, could not be a racist. And yet, to counter that, it might be all right to caricature a people (the Jews, the WASPs) who are treated in their complexity using a variety of characters, but why is the only black man in the novel a large stud who goes about humping frustrated white women, the Eskimos all smelly, and the only black character in his forthcoming novel a stereotypical hot black woman, and in the one following that, another black stud humping a white woman? Nevertheless, it could be argued that it is the hapless WASP, never quite sure of his guilty self, therefore easily manipulated, who is made the cruellest butt of Richler's satire. But this argument will not satisfy all critics.

This novel seemed to confirm Richler as a very Canadian writer when, according to his earlier declarations, he would rather be seen as just a writer. Even Jack McClelland had warned him about the "local" jokes; London's *The Tatler* called the book "a bizarre Canadian in-joke." Richler himself had had doubts about its worth. But he had been inspired to write it, he finished it, and this is what it was. Four years had passed since his last novel. He was thirty-two and, increasingly, time mattered. It may have seemed minor at the time, and certainly is, compared with *Duddy Kravitz;* but it has stood the test of time and it set the course for Richler's future role as a witty, ruthless, and fearless public commentator, especially on matters Canadian.

TO BRIAN MOORE, journalism was a compromise, "a dissipator of talent." There is some truth to that, though that depends also on the writer's temperament and need. Many writers avoid having children for the sake of their careers. Mordecai Richler had an abundance in his five. If he kept himself busy, scrounging desperately for money to support them, it is also true that his family was his sustenance and anchor.

Richler's relationship with Moore is a fine little twist in the story of Montreal's rich and varied literary culture; it is also the narrative of a friendship that began over a drink between two writers at the onset of their careers, only to end unhappily decades later when they had reached their pinnacles. Moore was ten years Richler's senior. An immigrant from Belfast, he started out in Montreal with the *Gazette* first as a proofreader, then a reporter. To make extra cash, in the early 1950s he began publishing pulp thrillers, some under his own name, others pseudonymously, though his ambition was always to write serious novels. It was at the Montreal Press Club, when Richler returned from Europe in 1952–53, that the two were introduced by William Weintraub. A three-way friendship began, though the older two seem to have been closer and exchanged greater confidences. Moore was married to Jackie Sirois, whom Richler already knew as a young pup from Sir George Williams College hanging around the older literary types. When Richler returned to London in fall 1953, already with an offer from Deutsch to publish his first novel, he invited the Moores to visit him and Cathy with their son.

Brian Moore, having finished his first serious novel, *The Lonely Passion of Judith Hearne,* set off for Europe the following March with a stopover planned for London. Something about Mordecai Richler seemed to have already irked Moore. Writing from the ship, which apparently had a few literary types on board, Moore began taking digs at Richler. "Many points in Mordecai's vocabulary have been revealed to me as jargon," he wrote to Weintraub. Negative observations such as these would continue. He stayed with Mordecai and Cathy at their flat in Hampstead, which he found dingy but not uncomfortable. He could never live in such a place, he wrote. Mordecai, he complained, was too concerned with money. There was a jibe at the younger writer's accent, his long hair, his dressing, and the Mandrake, the club they visited together. Later he took to calling Mordecai "the Bard" behind his back and to using a mock-Biblical style to refer to him—"the Bard is soon off to Israel"; "He saith England is fucked ..."; "Mordecai speaketh with a strong West Indian intonation which makes all conversations disconcerting...."

And yet, when Moore's *Judith Hearne* was undergoing serial rejections—it was turned down by at least ten publishers—Richler recommended it warmly to his editor, Diana Athill. She read it, liked the novel, and Brian Moore's career and reputation were made. It is possible that she would have read the manuscript anyway; but Richler had recommended it, and she read it only afterwards. *The Lonely Passion of Judith Hearne* became a literary sensation.

Writers are notoriously jealous creatures. A good review of a fellow novelist sinks the heart of many a scribe fretting over his own career and potential greatness. Therefore Richler's generosity toward a fellow novelist, at a time when he was still a novice and could have been more wary of competition, was admirable. It was a trait remarked upon by many who knew him. Brian Moore too was generally well liked. What could have needled him about Richler that erupted in this puerility, the occasional dart thrown behind the back of a writer whom he also called a friend? It could be lingering bitterness from the fact that Mordecai Richler, barely twenty-two, had been accepted by a London house with a novel that was, understandably, far from great, when Moore himself, ten years older, was still a reporter on the beat, writing pulp fiction for pocket money; and then the younger writer going on to greater glory, with less than masterpieces, and finally putting in a good word for him. It could be envy at the confidence and arrogance of a youngster who went away to became a writer and became one, through the kind of perseverance Moore himself was too old for, and sheer good luck. According to Diana Athill, their common editor for some years, Moore was not envious, he was more "respected" in England than Mordecai. This was later, however. Richler was better known in Canada, was almost a public figure when the two met again in Toronto at the Boxing Day party in 1960 and the restaurant dinner that followed. Moore, after all, was an immigrant or expatriate writer in Canada; his *Judith Hearne* was set in Ireland.

Well into the 1960s the friendship continued. Moore's letters to Richler were always affectionate, though not as mischievous as those to Weintraub—which used witty *noms de plume* for the addressee and author; and of course he had come to the Richlers' rescue with a generous loan. In 1962 he had found them a house at the summer writers' and artists' resort of Amagansett in Long Island, where he and Jackie were regulars. Moore had been Emma's godfather and that summer taught Daniel to ride a bicycle. He introduced the Richlers around. Mordecai would be remembered from that summer with his Schimmelpenninck cigar and a snifter of Scotch or a bull's-eye cocktail of beer and tomato juice.

Surprisingly, Mordecai seems not to have been aware of Brian's barbs. He would send Brian copies of his manuscripts or books, to which Brian sent honest comments, praising or criticizing. He disliked *A Choice of Enemies,* liked *Duddy Kravitz.* Brian Moore evidently considered himself the older and wiser and a superior writer, the more so because he did not see the need to debase himself with journalism. As he wrote once to Richler, who was then fretting about money,

"Biggest point of all is that, in my limited experience 'serious' work eventually pays much more than other stuff." One cannot help feeling that he must have been an unhappy man at heart. At some point starting in the late 1960s, Brian turned cold toward Mordecai, as he seemed to do with many of his friends. He was also no longer with Jackie.

Florence Richler, who liked Brian Moore and believed he too was fond of her, once said:

> Brian could be absolutely wonderful, but he was not the most generous of people. That may sound unkind, but it's true. I think there was always a lot of jealousy and Brian was always quite unkind about Mordecai. I think so, from very early days. And making easy derogatory remarks about Mordecai as a young man. I don't think he really thought he was a *novelist*. I think he hurt Mordecai very badly, although Mordecai did not show it. With Brian, those little daggers were never more than a quarter of a centimetre below the surface. And they were shot and thrown in every direction.

The two rarely met now, and if they did, at a common event such as a reading, it was the briefest of encounters. As Richler describes the last years of their relationship, in an article following Moore's death in 1999:

The last time I saw Brian was at the Booker Prize dinner in London in 1990. He had been short-listed for the third time, me, the second. Neither of us won, but that's not the point. We stood there, I feeling foolish and uncomfortable in my tuxedo, exchanging pleasantries awkwardly, which was a damn shame, because we had been the closest of friends for many years.... The last time I heard from Brian was when I was in hospital [in 1998] for some unpleasant surgery. It was a note wishing me well, and, in my vulnerable state, I shed a few tears for our foolishly aborted friendship.

The writing careers and styles of the two offer a study in contrast. Brian Moore did not spread himself thin writing journalism, though he did write some screenplays. He produced numerous works of fiction and became one of the most respected novelists of his time. Richler in his novels was the storyteller and explorer of Montreal's Jewish life; in that he had rewritten the Canadian novel; eventually he returned to live in Montreal because that was home and the source of his inspiration. Richler's style, too, was energetic, his language, as we have seen, deploying the inflections and the humour of the ghetto, reflecting its easy informality. It is acknowledged that Richler's women characters were weak.

Brian Moore was the opposite, his writing sparer, his women strongly painted and sympathetic. Ever the exile, he had left his native Belfast at the age of twenty-two and worked in Algiers, Rome, and Marseilles during the war years, and done a journalistic stint in Poland, before going to Toronto and then moving on to Montreal. Later he went to New York, and then California, though he never disavowed Canada. His novels are set in different places and in different periods. Almost as if he had his friend Mordecai Richler in mind, in a 1992 interview with the *Los Angeles Times,* he said, "I often wonder what would have happened to me if I had stayed in Ireland and written about my own world all the time. And I'm going to die now not knowing if I made a mistake or not." And throwing us a clue about his discomfort with Richler, he also voiced his suspicion of literary fame, calling it the angel of death. In Canada, meanwhile, it was questioned that Moore was even a Canadian novelist, an obsession periodically voiced by those apparently idling during writer's block, or old age, holding up the national flag.

WHERE WERE THE PROMISED Montreal novels eagerly awaited after *Duddy Kravitz*? St. Urbain Street, real and imagined, awaited their creative genius. Was Mordecai Richler dissipating his creative energies seeking exposure and fame, playing up to the Toronto gallery? His next work of fiction was a small novel, developed from what he had called the Shalinsky-Griffin novel, which became first "It's Harder to Be Anybody" and finally *Cocksure*. It was inspired by an experience related to him by Doris Lessing. Set in London's publishing world, *Cocksure* is a crisp and amusing satire of political correctness in its attitudes to sex, education, and race in 1960s England. The central character of the novel is Mortimer Griffin, senior editor at Oriole Press, originally of Caribou, Ontario, and hapless WASP. On the one hand, he's hounded at his weekly lectures at a local college by J. Shalinsky, who believes Mortimer to be a closet Jew, only ashamed of the fact; on the other hand, he's snarled at by Hy Rosen, his rival and "best friend" at Oriole Press, who believes Mortimer to be anti-Semitic and is ever ready to put up his fists to defend the cause of the Jews. No manner of protestation can satisfy either of Mortimer's persecutors. He is a liberal, who will bend over backward to prove—or protest—that he is not a racist or anti-Semitic. But the more he tries, the more he appears to incriminate himself. His wife Joyce, also an Ontarian, works appropriately and fashionably for the Anti-Apartheid League and Oxfam. Oriole Press is owned by the "saintly" Lord Woodcock, "a Fabian with the purest Christian motives." (Besides the pun, there is a dig here at George Woodcock, Canada's somewhat saintly man of letters, English born, whom Richler did not care for too much.) Ready to take over Oriole, a pillar of old English establishment, is the Star Maker, a tycoon from Hollywood, who sends to London his Italian-American henchman Dino Tomasso.

The book received some very positive reviews. In Canada it went on to win the Governor General's Award. It had its fans splitting their sides with laughter. Others found it stylish but slight, picking on easy targets without offering much in return. A spoof such as this may titillate for a time, delight those whose targets are hit, but runs the risk that its issues will become passé. And indeed, since the 1960s they seem to have become so. Extremes of political correctness are often laughable and annoying, and sometimes dangerous, but they come and go, and are as often based on legitimate issues. Speaking many years later, Richler's American editor, Robert Gottlieb, who was also a close friend, used for this and the previous novel, *The Incomparable Atuk,* the very appropriate term "japes." While he published this novel, Gottlieb was awaiting Mordecai's next major novel that the author was already struggling with.

CHAPTER SEVEN

Goodbye, London;
The Embrace of Canada

Over the years Mordecai Richler had continued to contemplate returning home. He had come back for brief periods, and made close friends and acquired ardent admirers (and furious detractors). He had sought employment, to enable him to stay, and when nothing steady came up, Canadian sources—CBC, *Maclean's,* and others—were ready to commission material from him, contributing to his sustenance abroad. He received grants from the Canada Council. His largest literary success, in terms of readership and celebrity, was also in Canada. His breakout novel was set in his native Montreal. There could be no question that he was a Canadian. In London, moreover, even though he was well known and had connections, he was one among many writers, including Americans, vying for attention. And as he well knew, America and things American have always held greater attraction for the British. Canada was Richler's home and inspiration; what he said had relevance there and was listened to; but he had been away too long. Already the occasional letter would arrive from an irate editor that he was out of touch with the country, he did not know what was going on. It must have hurt. A letter from Jack McClelland chided him, not without a note of under-standing, for choosing to go to Cannes over Winnipeg. Therefore, twenty-two years after he first left the country, in 1972 he decided to return to stay permanently. As he explained to Weintraub in a letter:

> The truth is I prefer living in London but, but, I fear for my novels. Looking around at others in my position ... [Dan] Jacobsen, [Doris] Lessing, [J.P.] Donleavy, even Brian [Moore], I fear the work is thinned by too long an absence from roots. I do not wish to consume my 40s writing histor-ical novels (Jacobsen). Or about imagined worlds (Doris). So honoring my "talent," I will return. So far the kids don't know....

This is a trauma that writers away from their homelands inevitably come to face, and cope with in their own ways— from Joseph Conrad, who wrote great novels, but never an "English" one, to Nabokov, whose America was singularly offbeat, to Joyce, who wrote about Dublin from Europe. Doris Lessing would of course go on to win the Nobel Prize for her work, of which only her early collection of stories was set in her native Zimbabwe. V.S. Naipaul, another colonial he had known, stayed on in England and also went on to win the Nobel Prize. But Mordecai Richler was hooked on Montreal; he was thoroughly North American in his sensibilities; and Canada would not let him go—unlike, it might be argued, Lessing's Rhodesia or Naipaul's Trinidad—however much he had mocked its provincial ways.

He had passed forty, was no longer young. There had been health issues: a false alarm for a heart attack, a recurring back problem that laid him up in bed. It was the time of life when a writer, older and domesticated, and battleworn, might begin to think of legacy, definition. What would he write for the remaining years of his life? What kind of writer was he? *Atuk* had been quirky, *Cocksure* not quite rooted. His recently completed novel, *St. Urbain's Horseman,* was rooted and major, its issues timeless. It would last. He knew it, everyone knew it. And it was Montreal, it was Jewishness, even though also partly London.

He would confess later to feelings of nostalgia about Montreal, even its winters, that had helped pull him home:

With immense excitement, I read about Montreal's historic 1972 blizzard, a two-day humdinger, cars abandoned everywhere, downtown streets impassable; the men, unable to make it home from their offices, consoling themselves in hotel bars; and snowmobiles displacing ambulances. Instead of being grateful to watch it on the telly, snug in my Surrey home, I felt deprived. I had also come to pine for sweltering summers and the mountain lakes of my boyhood. I sent home for seeds and planted Quebec Rose tomatoes in our greenhouse. They failed to take. Surely, an omen.

He himself had not taken much to the city that had given him his first break and nurtured his writing. Albeit with interruptions, he had spent half his life there, but he was too much a St. Urbain boy. He never learned to speak like the English. He did not develop an interest in cricket or football (soccer); British culture and politics remained peripheral to his existence. Baseball and hockey remained his passions, and he followed the league scores avidly across the Atlantic. One gets a sense throughout his writings that he did not care much for England, or English ways. The class system unsettled him. And so his close friends in London would always remain fellow expatriates. Of his novels set in England, one was about a set of expatriates, another was a spoof whose main characters were also expatriates.

Nevertheless, the move was not easy. His children were English in their ways, and Florence loved England. She never had any intention of returning to Canada. Now she had a stable home, a beautiful house, a life she loved. She would visit the theatre and the concerts, while Mordecai stayed with the children. (There was also a nanny.) They had their circle of friends, their social life, there was the children's schooling to consider. But the greater trauma was the prospect of uprooting, for someone whose first break in the continuity of her existence had been the knowledge that she had been adopted. She was unhappy with his decision, perhaps depressed and angry. With a family of six, you don't just pick up and leave. Richler knew the sacrifice she was making, giving up a life she knew and loved so he could go back to his roots. "The last thing she wanted was to marry someone who wanted to come back to Canada," he said. He worshipped her, their friend and his editor Robert Gottlieb said. And surely she reciprocated that devotion, she who went along with this departure from the life they had built, purely on his say-so, whose outcome they could not be completely sure of. Not that he did not have qualms. He had left

Canada with no regrets, he had said, and could recall the mediocrity and small-mindedness that he had escaped. "Literary London had been uncommonly hospitable. It was still exhilarating." They decided not to sell their house on Kingston Hill, just in case they had to come back.

It took Florence ten years to get used to her new life. Canada was quieter; the cultural life sparer and out of the mainstream of the Western world; the circle of friends less diverse and less challenging, less cohesive. The children, too, were uprooted. They were not consulted, having been given the impression that the move would be temporary. The youngest, Jake, was four years old; the oldest, Daniel, had to stay behind for a few weeks to take his O Level exams.

One morning, in the presence of their long-time friend Ted Kotcheff, they loaded their luggage into a car and set off for the Southampton docks. With them came the nanny. It was a sad moment. Richler for some reason brought out the family toaster and stomped on it, saying, "I always hated that toaster!" Was it the toaster or something else? Florence broke into tears. They arrived at the harbour and boarded the Soviet ship *Alexander Pushkin,* car and all, where in their cabin they gave a farewell party for their friends. Then they headed west to Canada on a voyage that would be remembered more for its bad food than anything else. As he strolled the decks, he could not help brooding on the wisdom of the move. "I wondered if I had left matters too late, if my return was ill advised, a sentimental and potentially costly form of self-indulgence."

Richler never regretted his return. As the years wore on, a mellower man and adulated by many in his native land, he would even criticize his previous attitudes to it as simplistic; but in the same breath, as it were, he always remembered the provincialism he had escaped more than once; and surely he was forgetting the freedom of being footloose in exciting Paris, and in Spain and in London, free to look back, find himself, and write.

And Florence, what did she brood about as the *Alexander Pushkin* skimmed the waves of the Atlantic, racing westward "home"? Surely it was to the needs of his literary inspiration she had given in, not to his nostalgia for Montreal winters and Quebec tomatoes and hockey. When his financial situation was better, he sent Florence to London to buy an apartment. It would become their wintering place; and two of their children would eventually return to make it their home.

A POSITION at Ottawa's Carleton University already awaited him upon arrival; he was required to be in the city only two days a week, coming in from Montreal, where the family rented a house in Westmount. The former St. Urbain's boy had gone full circle to return to live in his native city's poshest neighbourhood. It was not love for teaching that brought him to Carleton. He agreed to teach what he believed was the unteachable, creative writing, and he was neither a good teacher nor an encouraging one. He was brutally honest and, one imagines, somewhat grumpy. The students were in awe of him.

The two-year stint ended with his 1973 Plaunt Lectures at Carleton, in which he took up with gusto his role of national commentator and attacked his favourite target, "nationalist zealotry." Much of what he said was true. "I have warned students again and again that if twenty years ago Canadian writers suffered from neglect, what we must now guard against is overpraise." Obvious, but it often needs to be repeated in a country afraid it might run out of heroes. He excoriated those who would put a measure on Canadian content. (More than thirty years later, they still exist.) But he also overstated the case. "When, as is often the case, a Canadian novel is not published outside of Toronto, then the trouble is … that the novel is not good enough." Easily said, from his perch, but was it true? He acknowledged the frustrations of a writer not from Britain or America: "An American or British writer can lecture abroad and take it for granted that any literate audience will readily grasp what he is about." Even the non-literate audience, one might add, will identify more with an American or British novel; and potential sales, determined by the numbers of such readers, as Richler well knew, is what often largely determines publishability. He could hardly have denied that his great success was due to the Canadians' lavishing of praise on one of their own; in London or New York, he was after all just another writer. Even today, on Google, *Duddy Kravitz* comes up first as the name of a movie, whereas in Canada it is a celebrated novel. But Canada needed a vanguard against mediocrity, and fearless Richler was the man. A nation celebrating mediocrity renders all its artists mediocre in the world's eyes.

In that lecture, Richler in particular targeted the recently introduced government grants to Canadian publishers, though he favoured grants to writers. He himself had received Canada Council grants when in dire need in England. His argument against grants to Canadian publishers was that they discriminated against Canadian writers who published with the multinationals. One could counter that multinational publishers, with their deep pockets, could do enough for a Canadian writer with or without a grant. And if quality of writing was the question, it was the grants to authors that risked supporting the second-rate while always increasing the Councils' constituencies. Many years after the Plaunt Lecture, McClelland & Stewart, a Canadian company of iconic status and long Richler's publishers before he moved to Knopf, became partly owned by Random House, itself part of a global conglomerate that also owned his new company.

Richler's friend the publisher Jack McClelland, who disagreed with him about the issue of publishers' grants, recommended him in 1974 as the Canadian reader for the Book of the Month Club (BOMC). Richler was a diligent reader, and the critiques and recommendations he produced were often incisive. But he had to read dozens of Canadian books year in, year out, and though this job gave him enjoyable trips to New York, perhaps it was another sideline that took him away from his more serious writing.

OVER THE PERIOD of thirty years from his return up to his death, Mordecai Richler would publish only three full-length novels, though he also published the popular Jacob Two-Two children's books and several works of non-fiction. In his fiction he would go back to the Montreal milieu of his childhood and youth; this tendency to return to a past long left behind was something for which he had, in fact, faulted his London friends from the colonies. It was a symptom of a malaise, which to cure he had physically returned home to

Canada. In his successive novels Richler, however, would rework that imaginative world of his childhood to explore the situations of his protagonists as they grew older and went on their different ways. He became, in effect, the grand storyteller and mythmaker of St. Urbain Street, which had long since become transformed by new waves of immigrants, its former residents having moved on to wealthier Outremont or Westmount or farther on to Toronto during a climate of increasing instability and acrimony in the province.

His return did, however, give him material for his essays and columns—in effect, another literary career. Some of these pieces were personal; others were opinions and often satirical; a few took the form of travel writing, and some others were bagatelles, from a writer surviving on his craft and finally beginning to live off his reputation. Many of these pieces were brought out in collections. A proud professional, he had always used such occasional writing to supplement his income and even his lifestyle. He was an engaging, combative, humorous writer in this vein, and ironically it was through these shorter commentaries that many Canadians would come to know and adore him.

There grew, inevitably for a celebrated man of letters, an established quality to Mordecai Richler: he did the literary circuits, juried prizes, and critiqued for the BOMC; he wrote opinions that were often incisive and provocative. Gone were the urgency and the desperation, the excitement and fever of a young man on the brink of his career, sending off earnest letters to friends, family, and publishers, announcing his plans, celebrating the small and the large, asking for money. Inevitably, too, there appeared, in his columns, an element of playing to the gallery; he often said the unsayable, regarding Canadian culture, political correctness, and even occasionally the United Jewish Appeal, and this excited his friends and admirers, though one cannot help thinking that he sometimes took the short logical cut, going the straight line, unwilling to glance at the valleys, pay attention to nuances. It is the satirist's job to point out the ludicrous in certain positions, and Richler jumped at the chance whenever some enthusiast for a cause tripped over themselves without realizing it. He would thus become a proxy for the Canadian right, who came to embrace him, and for all those whose gut responses he seemed to be articulating so well.

The trajectory from working class and left wing in youth to the right in older age is a well-travelled one. But it would be incorrect to map Richler's career squarely upon it. What he consistently stood against, and ridiculed, was the special pleading, the hypocrisy, and the sheer opportunism that often lie behind trendy causes. But he was not one to explain himself, or build bridges, and one wonders if the perception of him as increasingly belonging to the right led to his distancing from his old leftist friends from London, George Lamming and Doris Lessing. According to a witness, at a Toronto festival in the 1990s, Lamming walked by Richler without even a nod; and Lessing mentions Richler only in a passing sentence in her autobiography.

Throughout his career, Richler had used material from his life in his novels; he also often wrote about himself, so that he produced a large quantity of autobiographical material, though not exhaustive and sometimes repetitive. He had no qualms about recycling material. In the personal writings we do find a story of his life, albeit patchy. Thus, he wrote affectionately about his father, but relatively little about his mother—though she appears fictionalized in several novels, an intriguing figure that one must discover for oneself. He never wrote about his first wife, Cathy; and about Helen, his girlfriend in Europe, he attempted a fictionalized account in the unpublished and aborted manuscript "Return to Ibiza."

IN LONDON, writing film scripts had rescued him from a life of near penury, with a new and growing family. He had a knack for it, yet he could not let it come in the way of his serious creative work. He turned down some tempting prospects. Back in Canada he was not as dependent on scriptwriting, and there were not many commissions forthcoming anyway. But in May 1972, a few months before he returned to Canada, in Cannes he had happened to meet three other Canadians, his old friend Ted Kotcheff, producer John Kemenyi, and Michael Spencer of the CFDC—the Canadian Film Development Corporation—and the idea for a film treatment for *Duddy Kravitz* was broached once more. It had come up a long time ago, in the 1950s, when the book was published. Ted Kotcheff had said he wanted to do it but over the years could find no one interested in financing a film about a Canadian Jew growing up in Montreal. Chicago, yes, New York, yes. But Montreal? Now, with the Canadian-government-funded CFDC willing to throw in support, a movie might just be possible. Richler's old nemesis, the CBC, demurred in giving any money to the project, but a former schoolmate called Schneider from Baron Byng came to its timely rescue. There were some difficulties, including a bad initial script, which Richler rewrote, and a financial shortfall—the budget had been set at $600,000 and ended up a little less than a million—before the movie was released, in April 1974, with well-known international stars and an upcoming Richard Dreyfuss in the lead role of Duddy Kravitz. Shooting was done on location in Montreal and at the Eastern Townships in the fall; reading Richler's account of the proceedings makes it too evident that he was in his element, he was home.

The film was launched in Montreal, as was appropriate and at Richler's insistence, at a black-tie charity event, $100 a couple. It went on to become the most commercially successful Canadian film to date, won the Writers Guild of America Award for Best Comedy Adapted from Another Medium, and the Golden Bear at the Berlin International Festival, and was nominated for the 1974 Academy Award in the category of Best Screenplay Adapted from Other Material. For Richler, the trip to Hollywood for the award ceremonies was, however, a journey to another planet. He went with Florence and seemed to have enjoyed it, the honour as well as the slights, for there was a pecking order in place dependent strictly on one's worth. At the airport they had not been met by limo or taxi; they stayed not at the posh Beverley Hills Hilton but their agent's flat; and so on. He managed to keep bemusedly detached from it all, however, and felt—one supposes—utter contempt at the vacuity and moral worthlessness of Hollywood. Ample supplies of liquor seem to have helped, and according to one witness he managed, on the Awards night, to utter an expletive at the actress Lauren Bacall a couple of seats away. He didn't have to go, of course. But why miss the experience? And he got an article from it, after all.

Flush with financial success, he was now able to afford a cottage for his family in the Townships, at beautiful Lake Memphremagog, which he liked to call his dacha. But it was no mere everyman's cottage, with its two floors and seven bedrooms, not to mention a sunroom. Soon he had a motorboat and he could be seen on the lake on a bright summer morn or warm evening taking it out for a spin. At cottage parties in this exclusive resort he might meet one or more of the high and mighties of the province, politicians, newspaper baron and future lord Conrad Black. This was a kind of life and prestige he could never have attained in England.

IN THE MID-1990s, twenty years after his return to Canada, he wrote about London—where he had begun to spend his winters with his "restless" wife—in an article titled "London Then and Now." A confirmed Canadian institution now, Mordecai Richler liked little about the city. He did not care about its cultural scene, sports, infatuation with royalty, the incestuous literati. "Alas, we had been in London for only a month when I realized that we had settled among vulgarians and that I would now have to endure cultural overload that could oblige me, any night of the week, to get into a suit and tie and charge out into the rain to attend one or another of the oppressive cornucopia of plays, concerts, or vernissages available.... A quick perusal of Time Out reveals the week's depressing choice of political demonstrations, lectures, gallery openings, museum special events, concerts, and plays." It is a middle-aged Richler writing, a man of the people, when he doesn't have to pretend to enjoy concerts, or feel obliged to support left-wing causes, or go to yet another avant-garde interpretation of Shakespeare or a performance of Benjamin Britten. Florence apparently did still patronize and enjoy those cultural events. He defends hockey, scorns soccer fans (when they were at their worst in England). He almost brags about his Canadianness. We know that he had begun to appreciate it more and more. In its simplicity was its sanity. But this diatribe against London is not one of his wiser moments, but of playing a role, writing too quickly for a deadline. One wonders what he would think about cricket reports in *The Globe and Mail* now and soccer attendance in Toronto matching hockey's. But he was not one to deny the passage of time; he would only be honest to his own.

CHAPTER EIGHT

The Haunted Jew

As a young man Mordecai Richler once said that he believed one should mourn those who died in the concentration camps because they were human, not because they were Jews. This was said in a letter, and was definitely not a considered opinion; it was, perhaps, only a working hypothesis by a young man. It is raised here only to remind us how engaged he was with the question of his Jewish identity. We should mourn people's tragedies not because of who they are—that sounds reasonable enough, though it's idealistic, going against the grain of common human behaviour, an attempt at a humanist point of view. One should grieve for all human suffering; but we grieve for family and tribe first. We can hardly be surprised at Jews mourning for Jews, following a history of anti-Semitism and exclusion. It was as Jews that the victims were selected.

What kind of a Jew was Mordecai Richler? In his fiction he invoked the community, always, but not its God. He did not seem to have believed in God as an adult, but he did not take Him on or blaspheme. In an unusual instance, however, in an article titled "Deuteronomy," he talks irreverently and even fondly of the God of the Bible, the author of so many of the inhibitions he grew up with. To illustrate the meaning of God to him, he tells a story about Evelyn Waugh and Randolph Churchill in a British plane about to be parachuted into Yugoslavia. Churchill, answering Waugh's challenge, picked up and started reading the Old Testament; halfway through, he slammed the book down, saying, "I never realized that God was such a shit!"

Says Richler, "I have repeated this anecdote often, though never in an airplane, because, such was my upbringing, the truth is it still scares me to tell it at thirty-five thousand feet."

Richler tells another revealing tale in the article. It is about his friend Ornstein from school.

> Ornstein, who broke with the Communist Party long ago, is still opposed to all kinds of religious mumbo-jumbo, any sort of tribalism. A scientist of some renown, he always seems to be heading for or just coming back from an important international conference in Tokyo, London or Milan. Last year he was in Jerusalem for the first time, and he went to see the Wailing Wall. "And you know what?" he said. "I burst into tears. I wept and I wept."

As a child Mordecai Richler attended the Talmud Torah Jewish parochial school, where Hebrew was taught in the morning and English and French in the afternoon. Moreover, coming from an observant Hasidic family, he went two afternoons a week to the Young Israel Synagogue for Talmud lessons. And even though the boys would make fun of the teachers and play pranks, many of those lessons were indelibly impressed on his mind, for he always relished quoting in his novels stories from the Bible and the arguments of the old rabbis; Moses Maimonides, "the Rambam," and Rabbi Akiva were his favourites. Back as a boy he could not switch on lights, listen to the radio, or answer the phone on Sabbath. This must have been deeply embarrassing, for not all his mates at the Talmud Torah came from such strictly observant families and he would get teased. On Saturday nights the family would gather at his grandfather's house for the ceremony of the ending of the Sabbath, when a candle would be lit and placed in the hands of the youngest child.

As a teenager, soon after his bar mitzvah, Mordecai started rebelling; he boasted about being an atheist, violated the Sabbath, and walked about bareheaded. His tyrannical grandfather, Shmarya, kept tabs on him and on several occasions beat him for non-observance while his timid father watched and suffered lectures. How frequently this happened is not clear, but on the last of these punitive occasions, before a tribunal composed of the entire family, Shmarya called the boy a *shabbus goy,* violator of the Sabbath, and slapped him about the face before throwing him out. The two never spoke again. Mordecai had become an *apikoros,* he says, an unbeliever. When the old man died, in accordance with his will, Mordecai, fourteen years old, was not allowed to touch the coffin. "I turned to my father. Help me. Help me," Richler wrote many years later. That he was so aggrieved by this denial to participate in a sacred ritual for the dead is revealing. A child wants to rebel, not to be thrown out.

Jewishness was all around him, in language, in customs, in history and memory. It saturated the air in that small grid of streets west of the Main called the ghetto. Like the proverbial burden of the Jews, Mordecai carried it with him, though not to lament it but to interrogate it. As a young man he had been tormented by his Jewish heritage and the question of assimilation; he had yearned to be simply himself. He went away not only from what he would call a provincial, "picayune" Canada, but also from a stifling community life confined to within less than a square mile, and its demands based on ancient traditions. His confrontations with his Jewishness would become the stuff of his fiction; its brilliance, close observation, and authenticity of atmosphere, character, and language would reflect his intimacy and even his affection for the community he grew up in. Indeed, in some sense, he never left it.

In another sense, though, he did break out. He married a non-Jewish woman against his family's strongest objections. By this time he had formulated his position as a Jew confidently enough to reply to his wounded father, sternly and unapologetically, telling him in effect that his father's (Shmarya's) God was from the Stone Age. His second wife, Florence, was also non-Jewish (though she had formally converted), and he did not raise his own children strictly as Jews. They were not bar-mitzvahed, did not visit synagogues. The home was not kosher. His daughters went to convent schools, for their quality of education, and his sons went to private English schools. But he enjoyed presiding over the Passover meal and going over the Biblical stories with the children. He also enjoyed playing Father Christmas, and leaving out stockings and presents for the children, concessions perhaps to a harmless winter holiday phenomenon and occasions for a pang or two of conscience. When his father died, he returned to Montreal for the funeral, but at the ceremony refused to have his tie and jacket cut, as tradition demanded. And finally, when he

himself died, he was buried in a non-denominational ceme-
tery in Montreal.

But it was for being a Jew that he could be denied access
to certain public places in his native Canada in the 1940s
and 1950s. He was well aware of why his grandfathers had
to leave Eastern Europe. Six million people who bore the
same brand as he did perished for no other reason than that
identity. You cannot become an un-Jew by rebelling against
it. Not only had he imbibed the tenets of Judaism from the
synagogue, the Talmud Torah, and the home; but also, as he
wrote to his father, he continued to study it. That a man
with such a complex, searching relationship with his origins
would be called a self-hating Jew is a case of the easy name-
calling that is so much a part of our recent culture; in his
case it is also touched by a cruel irony.

Richler strongly denounced the anti-Semitism he had
witnessed: among the teachers at Baron Byng, in the admis-
sions policies at McGill and Sir George Williams College,
and in the Quebec of the war years. In one major, and quite
uncharacteristic article, he systematically took on the anti-
Semitism in the works of Ian Fleming, the author of the
James Bond novels, which were so much a phenomenon of
1960s London.

But anti-Semitism, just as racism or sexism, can also be too easily invoked. Invoking it doesn't automatically put one on the side of the righteous. Richler, always brutally honest, was not one to ignore the humour latent in this situation. And so when as a boy he discovered his grandfather cheating a goy and reported to his father, Moe's response, after "What do you know?" was the lame non sequitur, "They're anti-Semites, every one of them." Similarly, the facile invocation of "the six million":

> The Holocaust, the most unspeakable act of our time, has undoubtedly been cheapened over the years by being invoked too frequently, sometimes as blackmail of a sort. Say by the plump Toronto suburban rabbi whom I once heard brandish it before his congregation in an appeal for funds for a new state-of-the-art temple-cum-community centre. Contribute big, he seemed to be saying, or you have spat on Anne Frank's bones. Or take my militant Zionist friend Ginsburg. Denied a choice table in the Ritz gardens or an upgrade on his flight to London, he will fire off a letter of complaint to the Montreal *Gazette,* saying, "Remember the 6-million."

The film *Schindler's List* by Steven Spielberg, Richler said in the article, was also a cheapening of the Holocaust, made in the same vein as the director's *E.T.* and *Jurassic Park,* trivial and predictable. A crowd-pleaser. Read Primo Levi, instead, he said, or Elie Wiesel's *Night* for authenticity and dignity.

The "unspeakable act" preyed on his mind as he pondered his heritage and its meaning to him; and despite his youthful pronouncement that it should be grieved in humanist and not communal terms, it affected him as a Jew. His creative response to it is the brilliant and complex novel *St. Urbain's Horseman.*

ON THE ONE HAND, the novel is about the middle, postwar "lost" generation that was left with no big causes to fight; the expatriates of *A Choice of Enemies* form one such group. In *Horseman,* however, that generation is represented by a descendant of Eastern European Jews, a former denizen of Montreal's ghetto. Richler's protagonist, Jake Hersh, now lives in London, a successful television director married to a shiksa, Nancy, with a family of three children. He should be happy in his career and home; but he is cursed with a burden, an overworked fantastic imagination in which he has taken up the cause of the Jews through his alter ego, Joey, a missing older cousin whom he has glorified into a hero.

Jake was seven when Joey arrived with his mother and his sister to stay in the neighbourhood in Montreal. Judging by his appearance Joey seemed to have made a detour through reform school. Four months after his arrival he disappeared. He reappeared a few years later, in a red MG bearing the stickers from many exotic places, before vanishing finally and mysteriously. Whether he was in fact a criminal or a hero, or both, is unclear, but to the boys of the ghetto who observed his daring exploits with awe during his second appearance, and especially to Jake Hersh, there is no doubt that he was a hero and defender of the Jews. His dashing arrogance and pizzazz easily stood out in the unassuming, working-class St. Urbain neighbourhood. "His fire-engine red MG looked so lithe and incongruous parked right there on St. Urbain, among the fathers' battered Chevies and coal delivery trucks, off-duty taxis, salesmen's Fords and grocery goods vans—the MG could have been a magnificent stallion and Cousin Joey a knight returned from a foreign crusade."

He stayed all of five weeks, during which he was observed sipping martinis with "high-quality" girls in his mother's backyard and driving off with a blonde in riding clothes. Not only could he ride horses, he also had a pilot's licence. He could easily stand up to the goys. It was 1943, Duplessis was premier, and anti-Semitism found open expression.

"Jewish shops were being broken and swastikas had been painted on the pavement outside the *shul* on Fairmont Street." The slogan "A bas les Juifs" had been painted on a highway. Anti-Semitic flyers were openly distributed. And Joey went around Jewish businesses exhorting the Jews: "What are you going to do about it?" One day he accompanied the St. Urbain boys to the playing field, where they were liable to face harassment from a gang of French toughs. The parents, who desired no altercation with the others, in the time-honoured way—what's a little bullying?—were not pleased. And then Joey disappeared; his MG was found turned over and gutted on the road to New York.

Jake eventually came to London, where he is now a successful television director. As the novel unfolds, he is on trial, falsely charged with the crimes of aiding and abetting sodomy, indecent assault, and possessing cannabis, having been set up by his co-defendant, a creepy, pathetic, and envious English Jew called Harry. Through his recollections during this ordeal, Jake's life is revealed, from his childhood in Montreal to his adult life in London as a secular Jew happily married to the shiksa—except that he is possessed by his Jewishness, haunted by the Horseman, Joey.

> Jake's past, which he had always taken to be characterized by self-indulgence, soaring ambition,

and too large an appetite, could at last be seen by him to have assumed nifty contours. A meaningful symmetry. The Horseman, *Doktor* Mengele, Harry, Ingrid, all frog-marching him to where he was to stand so incongruously, stupefied and inadequate, on trial in Courtroom Number One at the Old Bailey.

Josef Mengele was the all too real doctor who conducted human experiments at the Auschwitz concentration camp. Jake has traced the Horseman to a kibbutz in Israel, then to American and Canadian army camps in Germany, where he had apparently shown interest in the affairs of the Mengele family. Finally a woman named Ruthy contacted Jake in London; she had been engaged to Joey, who subsequently disappeared. It was through Ruthy that Jake met Harry, who became his nemesis, landing him finally at Old Bailey.

Jake's similarity to Mordecai Richler is more than incidental; they are the same age and their parents are separated; the father, a beloved character, dies of cancer at about the same time as Moe does. Jake, like Mordecai, has been to Ibiza; Jake, too, is married to a non-Jewish wife and is passionately devoted to her and their children. Portions of Jake's father's letter to him disapproving his marriage to the shiksa are taken verbatim from Moe's letter to Mordecai when he

married Cathy. (Though, if anyone, Jake's Nancy is mod-
elled on Florence.) The large Hersh clan bears similarity to
the Richler clan; just as Mordecai did, Jake goes to Montreal
for his father's funeral. And finally, Jake's mother, who happens to be visiting him during the ordeal of his trial, is too
much like Lily, overbearing in her love and possessiveness, a
love that moreover is not or cannot be reciprocated. Her plea
to her son at the airport, as she departs for Montreal, begging for his love, and her subsequent anger at his indifference, chillingly forebode Lily's last letter to Mordecai when
they broke up.

If the avenging Horseman, Joey, haunts Jake, so too does
the Holocaust, personified by the Nazi Doktor Mengele:

> Sometimes Jake wondered if the *Doktor,* given his
> declining years, slept with his mouth open, slack,
> or was it (more characteristically, perhaps) always
> clamped shut? Doesn't matter. In any event, the
> Horseman would extract the gold fillings from
> the triangular cleft between his upper front teeth
> with pliers. Slowly, Jake thought, coming
> abruptly awake in a sweat.

The refrain Horseman, Horseman echoes through the novel;
passages are quoted about the horrors of the Holocaust.

How could he still hate the Germans, Nancy asks one evening. Easily, Jake replies, recalling his recurring nightmare, "the terror that took him by surprise in his living room, striking only on those rare evenings when he brimmed over with well-being" in the bosom of his family.

> ... in Jake's Jewish nightmare, they come. Into his house. The extermination officers seeking out the Jew vermin. Ben is seized by the legs like a chicken and heaved out of the window, his brains spilling to the terrace. Molly, whose experience has led her to believe all adults gentle, is raised in the air not to be tossed and tickled, but to be flung against the brick fireplace. Sammy is dispatched with a pistol.

NINE YEARS AFTER *St. Urbain's Horseman,* in 1980—when Richler was already back in Canada—he published his next novel, as large and ambitious, titled *Joshua Then and Now,* in which he continues his treatment of Jewishness and the Holocaust, as experienced by his generation, anchored as they are by their childhood in Montreal's Jewish ghetto. That neighbourhood is all important; it provides the vision and the worldview of the protagonists and anchors those larger issues within the milieu and in a specific history.

Joshua Shapiro is the same age as Mordecai and Jake; like them, he goes off to London, where after an ardent pursuit he marries a WASP, to whom, as to his children, he is passionately devoted, and by whom he is indulged. The theme of the ardent pursuit of a WASP, his devotion and fear of losing her, occurs in both novels, as it does in Richler's last novel, *Barney's Version*. (Miriam in that novel is actually Jewish, but to this reader she is too much like the other two wives.) If one does not want to draw easy parallels, one might at least see it as a stand-in for a preciously bought secularism. Jake returns to Canada a decade before Mordecai did, however, and is a sportswriter. Like Mordecai, he has a cottage by Lake Memphremagog in the Eastern Townships, where much of the novel is set. Joshua's father is a former boxer and enforcer for a crime boss, and his mother, among other things, is a stripper; but behind these disguises the reader will easily discern the spectres of Moe and Lily.

Both Joshua and Pauline, his wife, a senator's daughter, have a past to deal with: hers a dark family history, his his stay in Ibiza. As the novel opens, Pauline is in hospital, having suffered a mental breakdown. Coping with this crisis, as Jake does with his in *Horseman*, Joshua recalls his life onward from his boyhood on St. Urbain. Being Jewish is very much on the mind:

Canadian-born, he sometimes felt as if he were
condemned to lope slant-shouldered through this
world that confused him. One shoulder sloping
downwards, groaning under the weight of his
Jewish heritage (burnings on the market square,
crazed Cossacks on the rampage, gas chambers, as
well as Moses, Rabbi Akiba, and Maimonides); the
other thrust heavenwards, yearning for an inheritance, any inheritance, weightier than the construction of a transcontinental railway, a reputation
for honest trading, good skiing conditions.

Joshua's childhood on St. Urbain sounds familiar from
the author's other books; it is in his adult life as resident of
Westmount and the cottage by the lake that the interest lies.
Through Joshua and Pauline we see the tension between the
arriviste Jew and the old-Canada establishment WASP. The
days of anti-Semitic discrimination are over. Here is how
Pauline recalls that revolution, as seen from the campus of
McGill, in the early days, presumably the 1950s:

> Then, all too swiftly, Kevin [her brother] was
> into law school, where their father was still a
> legend, and Kevin, just like the others, discovered
> the Jews....

[T]here were all those fierce, driving Jews, who didn't play by their rules, each one hollering "me, me, me." My God, they demanded space, lots of space, but they didn't even know where their grandfathers came from.... [T]hey were not going to be denied....

"Oh my, all those short, dark men with heated black eyes. The appetite."

As elsewhere in Richler, for example in *The Incomparable Atuk* and *Cocksure,* the WASP male comes across as weak and effete. When Jake, in *Horseman,* needs a respectable lawyer, for example, we are told, in Jake's voice, "Say what you like about the *goyim,* they had their uses. For his defense Jake required an upright plodding WASP...." The Jew is aggressive, excitable, and full of appetite; you cannot fool him; son of a cobbler, a tailor, a plumber, or taxi driver, he is now a heart specialist, a psychologist, a dean at a university. A nouveau riche, with a house in Westmount, a distinguished wine cellar, a painting by A.Y. Jackson. Prone to heart trouble as he is in his stressed life, for he is a family man—"the children, the children"—he has a former classmate to consult. A life not unlike that of many immigrants today. "Survival" may have been the ethos of the WASP in Canada, but for these newcomers, it simply doesn't hold.

Joshua is bugged by his memory of Ibiza, and the unfinished business he believes he left there. Like his author, he had met a German, a "Nazi," called Dr. Dr. Mueller in this book. Mueller, older, suave, and perhaps better-looking than the former ghetto urchin Joshua, loves to needle him, taunting him with "Are you a man or a mouse?" Joshua, too conscious of being a Jew, and of the German's possible Nazi connections, hates him. He hates him especially for treating with contempt the other Jews in the town—a couple called the Freibergs, who escaped Germany after Kristallnacht and now run a hotel; Max, a peddler; and Carlos, whose family had remained Jews in secret since the Inquisition in Spain. When a pretty girl called Monique comes to the island accompanied by her mother, and prefers Joshua to the German, the latter connives to get the younger man deported. This circumstance bears a close resemblance to Richler's own adventures in Ibiza, and Monique resembles Helen. As Joshua hastily departs, he has nothing but contempt for himself. "Run, Joshua, run. You're not a man, but a mouse." He has abandoned Monique, and he has abandoned the Freibergs, who it appears will lose their hotel. Above all, he has let Dr. Dr. Mueller get the better of him. German against Jew.

But thirty years later when he finally goes to Ibiza, the Jewish avenger, it is apparent that he has followed a ghost:

> If Ibiza had changed and grown incredibly, the San Antonio he had known simply didn't exist any more. It was gone. In place of the sweet, somnolent village there was a thrusting resort town ... with a paved esplanade, elegant shops, a huge yacht basin, and an endless run of large hotels. Nobody could possibly walk into the sea and hunt fish from this waterfront any more

or make love on the beach to a girl like Monique. His old friend Juanito, who first welcomed him upon arrival, is now a toothless grandfather forbidden to drink by his doctor. The secret policeman who told him to leave town has recovered from a stroke, laughs at the frivolity of the past, and requests a copy of *Hustler*. Mueller is dead, and where his villa had been, now there stands a condominium building. And the Freibergs had long sold their hotel for a profit and departed.

The trip has been for nothing, except for the realization that the past cannot be reawakened. Joshua sets his watch to Montreal time, calls Pauline on the phone, and departs. There is a home, with matters to attend to there.

IT WAS WHEN he was in his sixties that Mordecai Richler took on his relationship with Israel. He had first visited the Jewish homeland in 1962, when he produced a series of three articles for *Maclean's*. Thirty years later he revisited it and wrote *This Year in Jerusalem,* in which as an older, mellower man, his engagement with Israel is more substantial and serious. The tone of this book is thoughtful and searching; it is as if, now that he is past his middle age, some confessions are in order, and the author is ready to acknowledge this part of his heritage.

Richler's involvement with Israel and Zionism began with his recruitment, in his first year of high school, into Habonim, a Zionist youth group with a socialist or collectivist ideological bent. The Habonim reflected the aims of its parent party (which boasted among its members David Ben-Gurion) to establish a Jewish state in Palestine. On Friday evenings the group members would meet at a house on Jeanne Mance Street to discuss and celebrate this homeland, where a glorious struggle was under way to establish it in the face of British and Arab opposition. They extolled the idyllic lives of the Jewish pioneers, sang romantic and inspirational songs in Hebrew or Yiddish, and discussed passionately the heroism of the Jewish fighters. Menachem Begin was their own Jimmy Cagney. On Sundays they would go fundraising door to door.

Richler maintained that he joined Habonim primarily for the girls, which sounds appropriately Richlerian but cannot be the complete truth. Even before Habonim, during Talmud Torah days, he says he would playact fighting for Israel with an imaginary gun. Later he became so wholeheartedly involved with Habonim that, pretending to be over eighteen, he joined the Reserve Army based at Montreal's Black Watch Armory, where on Wednesday nights he wore a uniform and learned to handle a gun.

> Habonim converted me into a zealot for Zion. I demonstrated. I badgered my aunts and uncles to join a boycott against British goods. I put in hours on our Gestetner, churning out propaganda that could be handed out on *goyish* street corners.

When the United Nations General Assembly voted in November 1947 for an end to the British Mandate in Palestine and the partition of the territory into Jewish and Arab states, there was wild celebration among the Jews. "Many wept as they sang 'Hatikvah,' the Zionist anthem. In New York, members of Habonim and Hashomer Hatza'ir joined hands to dance a hora in front of the *New York Times* building. In Montreal, we gathered at the house on Jeanne Mance Street, linked arms, and trooped downtown singing 'Am Yisrael Hai' (The People of Israel Lives)...." He adds:

> ... in that time of moral certitude, a two-thousand-year-old dream fulfilled, I was, like the other *chaverim,* insufferably condescending to our peers in the neighbourhood. They seemed ... so blind ... spending long nights studying for their university entrance exams, plotting future careers as doctors, dentists, lawyers, and notaries in what we scorned as the wasteland of the Diaspora.

Not surprisingly, then, his final-year results from Baron Byng were not so great and he had to settle for Sir George Williams College—where, however, life took on a completely different turn. While his friends from Habonim eventually made *aliyah* (emigrated to Israel), he made his pilgrimage to Paris.

Israel for Richler was not a simple issue. It had its contradictions and it raised troubling questions, as it did for many Jews. Would one rather live in Israel, the Jewish homeland, or in Canada (or the United States)? What indeed is a homeland? *This Year in Jerusalem* has two epigraphs, one a quote from a 1947 resolution of Habonim, which concludes:

> The New Eretz Israel calls upon us. Let us go and rebuild Zion. Our help, our support, our selves are needed.
>
> Let us arise and rebuild!

The other epigraph is from a statement made in 1938 by Albert Einstein, which is far from the Zionist position.

> I would much rather see reasonable agreement with the Arabs on the basis of living together in peace than the creation of a Jewish state.... I am afraid of the inner damage Judaism will suffer—especially from the development of a narrow nationalism within our own ranks.

What, then, was Israel to Mordecai Richler? There was not quite the choking moment when he arrived for the first time, in 1962, to the Promised Land of his ancestors. He was not a Zionist any longer. He was thrilled, nevertheless, walking that first night in Tel Aviv, "where everybody was like you, where you couldn't be goy-frightened into behaving larger than your true self or be put down for failings other than your own." If he no longer quite believed in a two-thousand-year promise, this was still a country where the Jews were a majority and Hebrew was spoken in the streets. He did not exult long over this. He was a tough young writer who had come to report.

Thirty years later the feeling is different. Israel now is to experience, in all its multiplicity, without coherence; it is to observe and listen to, in its many voices; it is to meditate over. It cannot be otherwise.

Having denied coherence, the resulting book is therefore scattered in its approach. Being in Israel has taken him back to his Orthodox Jewish upbringing, about which he muses in a manner he has not quite done before—it's not something he has escaped but a part of him; he comes up with quaint little childhood episodes he had forgotten or never written about before. Grandfather Shmariyahu, whom he had regarded a petty thief, comes to mind, not negatively this time, and the other grandfather, Rabbi Jehudah Rosenberg, drawing a picture of a man on a horse, wearing a wide hat in the manner of a Hasidim; he is led to puzzle over the bizarre politics of the Israeli nation with its multiple factions; he dwells on the contentious political history of the land; he describes his meetings with Montreal friends from Habonim who had made *aliyah* (when he hadn't). He meets Canadians and Americans, with whom he shares a North American Jewish culture and past. He treads gingerly, sensitivities are high. He does not presume to judge; if there is irony or satire in what he reports, it is of the mildest form. Throughout, he is seen by the Israelis he meets as a familiar, a fellow Jew and one of them, and also as a stranger, a North American against whom there runs a current of resentment and envy. "Do you own an aeroplane?" asks a taxi driver. There is not that much to see in Israel, unless you are a Bible scholar, but a lot of talking to listen to. A cacophony of opinion, a tangle of detail.

One of the most moving moments in the book is Richler's meeting with his former Habonim leader Ezra Lifshitz, whom he has not seen in four decades. Ezra, a former McGill engineering student, made *aliyah* in 1952, arriving at Kibbutz Urim, in the desert, near Gaza. As Richler describes it, not a pretty place and a very far cry from Westmount, where he only recently lived, and his large multi-room retreat in the Eastern Townships by Lake Memphremagog. Kibbutz Urim has six hundred members who work six days a week in their fields or in their mills, and have communal meals in, when Richler discovers it, "an unpleasantly hot dining hall, just about everybody in shirts and shorts and sandals, everybody helping themselves to food out of long metal trolleys." Ezra is sixty-six and works from eight to four every day at the textile mill, even though he doesn't have to, but just to be useful. "Do you ever yearn for Montreal?" Mordecai asks. "If somebody offered me a million bucks," comes the reply, "I wouldn't go back. I wouldn't know what to do. Here I'm part of something." He doesn't know how much he is paid, but he is sure he is in the black. He supports a Palestinian state. "Poor bastards have nothing. In Gaza you could probably sell a five-year-old toothbrush...."

When he returns to his room, having spent a night at the kibbutz, Richler reports to Florence that he has never been in the presence of so many good souls before—or eaten such unspeakably bad food. And he tells her Ezra's last words to him: "I've been here forty years last March, and I still believe in it."

He meets Sol and Fayge, two other former Habonim Montrealers, who made *aliyah* in 1950. "The dream has gone sour," Sol says at one point but does not elaborate. He later adds, "You're sitting and listening to the radio and you're fighting Scuds with Sellotape." All their children fought in the 1973 Yom Kippur War. Sol works for a support group helping runaway kids from ultra-Orthodox families. Richler observes, as he recalls this meeting at an Israeli-Arab restaurant: "It didn't strike me until later that neither Sol nor Fayge had asked me any questions about Canada, or about how Montreal had changed since they had left it forty-two years before. Difficult as it was, I had to accept that in some ways Canada was now the irrelevant Old Country for them, the way Galicia was for my grandparents."

Waiting for his cousin Benjy at a restaurant in Little Italy, sipping a much-needed Scotch, he is led to brood over the memory of the tyrant, his grandfather Shmariyahu. It was Benjy's father, Uncle Joe, who had told fourteen-year-old Mordecai he could not touch his grandfather's coffin. Benjy made *aliyah* in 1960. When Richler during his 1962 trip asked Benjy why he left Canada, Benjy had replied that he believed all the Jews would have to leave Canada. "It's not our country." Just the other day, at the Kibbutz Urim, a group of kids had asked Richler would he come to Israel if there was a Holocaust in America. Now Benjy is assistant director at the Jewish National and University Library, working with ancient manuscripts. Still very much a religious Jew, he gives Mordecai a long and interesting lecture on his work. When they part, he presents Mordecai with two books: one, Benjy's own beautifully illustrated *Hebrew Manuscripts: A Treasured Legacy,* inscribed, "To Motl, from Benjy, This is what keeps me going." The other, "compounding my pleasure," Richler says, a recently published Hebrew edition of his grandfather Jehudah Rosenberg's tales of the Golem and the Maharal of Prague. Lily would have been pleased too.

Throughout his stay, there comes news of terrorist killings. A computer expert bludgeoned to death at a Jewish settlement in Gaza; a Jew stabbed at a bus stop; a woman of fifty-seven stabbed five times in the back.

But Richler does not stop here. He visits a Palestinian refugee camp. It is a mark of his honesty, and indeed his courage under the circumstances, that in the Palestinian faces he also sees Jewish faces; that even as he feels a tug of sympathy for the Arabs, he recalls the historical oppression of the Jews. When his Palestinian Christian guide, an articulate young woman, shows him her old family house, now lost, saying that her grandfather still keeps the keys to it, Richler recalls that Spanish Jews expelled by the Catholic monarchs in 1492 had held on to their keys for generations. When a grieving Palestinian woman tells him, "The Jews haven't suffered as we have. We fight with stones. They have guns. Many of our children have lost their fathers," Richler recalls his grandfather Shmariyahu, sitting on his balcony catching the breeze on Jeanne Mance Street, *Der Kanader Adler* on his lap. "Was he, I now wondered, sitting out there pondering the fate of those Reichlers left behind in Rawa Ruska?" Where they perished during the war.

I ran through this heritage of outrages and endurance in my head, not forgetting the 1903 pogrom in Kishinev.... Or the Black Hundreds, the notorious Russian nationalist movement, perpetrators of innumerable pogroms, that emerged in 1904. Or Kristallnacht.... Or the conference at Wannsee that led to the Final Solution. But, even sending buckets down the well of my Jewish provenance, I still had to allow that Nihad 'Odeh and Aba Nidal Abu 'Aker were not culpable. They could not be blamed. Big-bellied, black-eyed [Aba Nidal]—endlessly rocking, keening, but also relishing the importance that injustice had bestowed on her, rendering her the mother of a martyr, was unnervingly reminiscent of the St. Urbain Street grandmothers of my boyhood, spinning their sorrowful tales of the Old Country. Instead of drunken Cossacks wielding swords, it was IDF delinquents with dum-dum bullets. Even as I luxuriated in guilt, I had to acknowledge a deeper feeling, one that I hadn't plucked out of my liberal convenience store. I was grateful that, for once in our history, we were the ones with the guns and they were the ones with the stones. But, taking it a step further, I also found myself hoping that if Jerry, Hershey, Myer, and I had been born and bred in the squalor of Dheisheh rather than the warmth of St. Urbain, we would have had the courage to be among the stone-throwers.

Israel, Jerusalem, then was a necessary journey, one of coming to terms and making peace with the ancestors and with his childhood. At the end of the journey, recalling Ezra, who would not leave for a million bucks, Richler concludes, "I too continue to feel a part of something, and at home, right here in Canada."

What we do not learn is why Richler did not look up Ezra on his first visit.

PHILIP ROTH'S WRITER-PROTAGONIST, Nathan Zuckerman, in *The Counterlife,* makes an eloquent case for why for some Jews at least, America (and by extension Canada) is the promised land.

> I was the American-born grandson of simple Galician tradesmen who, at the end of the last century, had on their own reached the same prophetic conclusion as Theodor Herzl—that there was no future for them in Christian Europe.... Insomuch

as Zionism meant taking upon oneself, rather than leaving to others, responsibility for one's survival as a Jew, this was their brand of Zionism. And it worked.... I could not think of any historical society that had achieved the level of tolerance institutionalized in America or that had placed pluralism smack at the center of its publicly advertised dream of itself.

Philip Roth is an interesting comparison to Mordecai Richler. Only two years younger, he too came of Galician grandparents and was brought up in a Jewish neighbourhood, Weequahic, in Newark. We recall that, but for a whim, Richler's paternal grandfather could well have ended up in New York (or Chicago). Roth too attended Talmud Torah as a child. His upbringing, however, was not as strictly Orthodox. His father worked at an insurance company in the city, and Roth himself ended up going to university and even graduate school. His characters are profoundly Jewish, though they negotiate this identity in personal terms as Americans. Roth in his fiction is deeply engaged with America, most obviously in the titles *The Great American Novel, American Pastoral,* and *The Plot Against America.* Richler was doubly exiled: a Jew in Montreal, a Canadian in Europe. Canada did not give him as grand a subject as

America did to Roth, but Jewishness did. Also interesting to note is that in *The Counterlife,* when Roth's Zuckerman goes to Israel, Arabs are background, though of course a vital one. Richler on the other hand goes to meet them, and he sees himself in them, without doing violence to his own history. Roth through his fictional character intellectualizes the predicament of Israel for an American Jewish writer, and he does so brilliantly. For Richler, Israel is not an intellectual journey but a personal one.

CHAPTER NINE

"Maw" and Mutkele

In the early 1970s, in Montreal, Mordecai Richler's mother, Lily, informed him that she did not wish to see him again. Their relationship had ended. Richler, as we have seen, kept his inner life private; even Florence was only occasionally privy to it. So we can only conjecture about the mother-son relationship based on external evidence. By the more simplistic accounts of the story, she was a typical Jewish mother, an evil witch in his life, or both. She was actually a complex and troubled woman, both interesting and accomplished, as well as a dominating mother. She was not well liked.

Lily's problem was that she had been married off to a very simple soul and a congenital loser, Moe Richler, for whom she very soon developed contempt.

> As younger, more intrepid brothers and cousins began to prosper, he assured my mother, "The bigger they come, the harder they fall."

My mother, her eyes charged with scorn, laughed in his face. "You're the eldest and what are you?"

Nothing.

All this humiliation the boy Mordecai watched. Surely he also felt some of his mother's contempt for his father? "As a boy, I made life difficult for him. I had no respect ... I was charged with appetite, my father had none. I dreamed of winning prizes, he never competed." His grandfather Shmariyahu would scold and hit Mordecai; his father only muttered empty threats.

During the war, some five thousand Jewish refugees were allowed into Canada. Many of them headed for Montreal, and one, Julius Frenkel, tall, erudite, and charming, came to live as a boarder with the Richlers. Lily had an affair with him, which could not remain a secret from Moe or the neighbourhood. She even wrote love letters to him, which Moe discovered. And unbeknownst to his mother and her lover, young Mordecai once discovered them in the act of sex. This had a profound effect on the boy, but reticent as he was, he confronted his mother with it only many years later, and also mentioned it to his brother Avrum.

Lily had her marriage annulled, and Moe left to live in a rented room—"Stunned, humiliated. St. Urbain's cuckold."

When Moses Richler died in 1967, Mordecai came from London for the funeral. Afterwards he wrote a moving tribute to his father that he reprinted in his collection *Home Sweet Home,* and which he read publicly with barely suppressed emotion. In that tribute, in his reading of it, one gets a sense of lost time. Moe, his humiliated father, did not get his due, his son was not there for him. It seems one of those instances when the son sees the father as a man, sees himself in his father:

> So many things about my father's nature still exasperate or mystify me.
>
> … was he really so sweet-natured as not to give a damn? Finally, there is a possibility I'd rather not ponder. Was he not sweet-natured at all, but a coward? Like me. Who would travel miles to avoid a quarrel. Who tends to remember slights—recording them in my mind's eye—transmogrifying them—finally publishing them in a code more accessible than my father's. Making them the stuff of fiction.

In confronting his dead father, the son finally gives us a rare glimpse of his own soul.

But Lily received no such tribute (though Mordecai's ambition reflected hers). He did not even attend her funeral. What happened?

She brought him up, a typical Jewish mother, diligently paid attention to his education, and always earned her living, most commonly by keeping rooming houses. She, as well as Moe, had sent money and food parcels to Mordecai in Europe the first two years. She was always proud of him. But unlike Moe, unlike Mordecai, she was effusive in her attentions. Overbearing. Too much.

Mordecai had loved his mother once, as he admitted some time after the break: "I was very close to my mother for a certain period." In his early autobiographical novels, the unpublished "The Rotten People" as well as the published *Son of a Lesser Hero,* the mother, already an overbearing figure even from a distance, is nevertheless and naturally guaranteed her son's affection. When Richler was settled in London, he would bring Lily to visit, and he would send money to her in Montreal. In his letters to William Weintraub, he referred to her as "Mum" and even "Mumsy." (Though when he wrote to her, he began "Dear Maw.") He kept her informed of his successes. When he returned to Montreal from Europe the first time, it was with her that he initially stayed. She was "Maw," after all.

Until, as he said, "she became insufferable." Until he was married again and bringing up a family of his own, a not untypical condition for family conflicts. When she came to visit, she tended to be bossy, aloof from Florence, her gaze, her attentions directed only toward her "genius" son. In Montreal the children would go visit their grandmother, watch TV, were fed, and the parents would later come by to fetch them. If she bribed them with presents in exchange for their affection, as has been suggested, that's hardly unusual in a lonely grandmother and deserves pity if anything. But there was a trigger that turned off the son from the mother. Perhaps something was said by the irrepressible woman, to Mordecai, to Florence. But according to Richler, it was simply that

> She was driving me crazy. She would turn up unannounced at seven in the morning.... [S]he wanted to move in, and I thought, "I won't be able to live here." So it was a question of survival, and I chose mine. It must have been 1974.

He sounds like a son with a parent. When she told him she didn't want to see him again, he said a silent Amen. Perhaps this was his way of travelling the mile to avoid a quarrel, or recurrent scenes. She died at the home of her older son Avrum, who would recall her in the most hateful terms. But, as he said, it was Mordecai who had been her favourite. And Mordecai himself sometimes had not thought highly of Avrum, to put it mildly.

The comic book scenario of Lily's dramatic conflict with her son has Mordecai as a latter-day Jacob Two-Two battling the Hooded Fang. It misses out on Lily's own story. She was not only a mother, after all. She would say that if she had been a boy she would have trained as a rabbi. That surely is a clue to her frustrations. A person trapped in a woman's body, by time, by Orthodoxy—for if she took pride in her religious tradition, it also kept her in her place—a mother, a daughter.

Not only did she write the quaint stories about a rabbi's household, with titles such as "I Pay a Visit to the Beloved Rabbi," she also wrote, in her seventies, her autobiography, *The Errand Runner*. It is a fascinating, informative book. We learn that much as she loved her father, she never forgave him for not letting her go on to high school, despite her teachers' entreaties on her behalf; and for falling for Shmarya Richler's wiles and arranging her marriage to his son. In Toronto, where her family first settled, she would accompany her father to circumcisions (and witnessed boys throwing stones at him because in his Orthodox rabbi's garb he looked so alien), and in Montreal to kosher inspections. She ran errands for him. According to her, Rabbi Jehudah Rosenberg had already discerned little Mordecai's Talmudic mind.

Her letters to her son until the early 1960s are missing, except for a handful, which are remarkable. Beginning "Darling Muttkele,—" her thoughts and emotions pour out in them in dense single space. We can understand his dread. She planned to read *Son of a Lesser Hero* three times, she wrote once, first as an ordinary reader, then as a mother, and finally as a Jew. Meanwhile, there followed a mini review. She defends the mother in the book (based on her), and understands that Mordecai may have hated her at times, just as there were times when she had hated her own father whom she also loved. She likes the portrait of the Jews (which had offended many of them). "The people who can think will enjoy it. Many parts of the book I mean. But as Cathy [Boudreau] wrote to me, it is not a pretty book. But life on St Urbain was not pretty and life for us was not pretty...." She can't help taking a dig at Moe, however, calling him pathetic.

In a breathless unpunctuated letter, except for dashes, she writes to "Muttkele" about reading Lucretius and Lillian Ross, and watching *The Red Badge of Courage,* and she mentions

Gide. In 1959 she confesses that she has met a Dutch Jew to whom she is attracted; they have spoken, sex has been discussed, but he remains secretive. Mordecai seems to have replied that this is "not kosher." Lily gives up the man after a few weeks. She goes to New York and sees a triplet of plays by Yiddish playwrights, Aleichem, Peretz, and Seforim: "they lost much in translation." She finds an African ballet "fabulous." She forms a literary club, plans a marriage bureau.

In the 1960s, when Florence is in the picture, the letters, which are preserved, are addressed to both her and Mordecai. She sends gifts to the children. She writes every week, preferably on Monday, and even when she says she's being short, the letters are long and dense; and articulate. She is disturbed by the Kennedy assassination. But, watching Martin Luther King's speech, she says, "I am beginning to weary of all the fuss made of Mrs. Kennedy, I can never forget the picture of Mrs. Evers [wife of civil rights leader Medgar Evers] as I saw and heard her speak on television after the brutal murder [1963] of her husband."

All this can hardly be dismissed as pretense, though no doubt there was a need to impress. But she was too much for a son with his own life and family. He did not want to discuss culture with her. He did not want a mother who was a colleague and a reviewer. But she needed a companion.

Richler perhaps saw greater honesty in the letters of the simple Moe, who was more the traditional father, even in his rejection of Cathy. His letters were short, with family news—"Sara's father died. Should you wish to send a card …"—and clippings, sometimes, containing news about Mordecai. Mordecai in his "Dear Daddy" letters sent stamps, once some Churchill commemorative coins, and mostly news about his own work. Moe did not presume to judge Mordecai or mention his work. It is not even clear that he had read them through. Once, in 1959, he wrote a mild note of admonishment. "The reviews [of *Duddy Kravitz*] are very good, but all critics mention the fact of certain language that could have been omitted," Quoting from the Ethics of the Fathers, he said the critics were the teachers and perhaps Mordecai could learn from them.

He lived, then, in a completely different cultural world from that of his wife or son.

IN THE MANUSCRIPT of Richler's first unpublished novel, "The Rotten People" (1951), the protagonist Kerman receives a letter from his mother that reads, in its tone and density, remarkably like one of Lily's. This is how Kerman responds to it in his mind, giving us a hint of the oppressive weight of his mother's attentions on a young Mordecai Richler:

> He felt as if he had been hunted down; over two
> continents and across an ocean, she was boring her
> clamps into him.... Then he felt a whole wave of
> conflicting emotions: his love for his mother, guilt
> for not having written her for so long, anger
> because she was going on furnishing a room for
> him.... A poisonous rage filled him to the brim as
> he visualized his insignificant brother—the
> nonentity of nonentities....

Kerman's view of his brother here is also worth noting.
Did Mordecai already dislike his brother at that early age
(twenty-one)? Much later he had made it clear that he did
not like Avrum. The reason was that Avrum had been borrowing money for his debts from the hard-pressed Moe, who
had to dip into his savings. My other disease is Avrumitis,
Moe said. When Moe was in hospital, seriously ill, he complained that Avrum was neglecting him. But it was Avrum
who had always been physically closer to Moe, and this was
Mordecai's guilt and later grief.

The harshest caricature of Lily in Richler's novels is as
Mrs. Hersh, Jake's mother, in *St. Urbain's Horseman,* who
comes to visit him and Nancy in London during his tra-
vails. It is evident that the watchful, interfering Mrs. Hersh
is Nancy's own travail, while Jake does his best to avoid his

mother. Dare we read in these scenes the domestic situation as it prevailed when Lily visited Mordecai and Florence? Perhaps. A letter written to the couple from Montreal ends thus, giving us a flavour of Lily's presence in their lives: "Mordecai, next time you write me, please dear put the pictures in the envelope first before you put the letter in."

Lily was aware of her caricature as Mrs. Hersh, and once complained bitterly about it.

The break between mother and son came in 1974 in Montreal. In a letter dated August 1, in which she returned his check for $500, she said she had been the object of "humiliation, insult and many times hatred"

> ... you are right ... I call you late at night, I interfere in your family life, I tell you how ill I am, I demand money from you. And I want to devour you with love. So I have decided never to trouble you any longer.

She does not want to see him again; his memory is her coat of many colours in exile.

But later she did send him some taped messages, to which, on August 3, 1976, he sent her a long, angry, and final letter of reply. It is accusatory, and he cannot help his sarcasm—about what he saw as her piety and pretenses—nor his contempt for her. Unfortunately, it cannot be excerpted or paraphrased here. "Dollink Muttkele," as she called him in another letter, concludes with a bombshell. A sin of the distant past—her sexual infidelity with the boarder Frankel—comes to haunt this woman now in her seventies. This much can be said: the letter is the one piece of evidence we have of how haunted Mordecai had been since the age of twelve upon witnessing the infidelity. It tells us why he found his simple father more authentic. What Mordecai saw one night in the bedroom he shared with Lily he told his brother Avrum, who reported it in an interview with Michael Posner in blunter and cruder terms than Mordecai himself used with his mother.

It must have crushed her, this letter. But surely it also pleased her a little? He was the old rabbi's progeny, after all. But in the letter it is also evident that there is no love left to spare for her. There is no room to forgive.

CHAPTER TEN

Engaging with Canada

In his youth Mordecai Richler's experience of Canada was essentially that of downtown Montreal. Before he left for Europe, he had been to Toronto and Ottawa once, and to New York to visit a contact. It was from New York, and the United States, that much of popular culture came to Montreal's Main: comic books, films, books and magazines, even the strippers at the Gayety; there were the fiery wartime anti-Nazi broadcasts by Walter Winchell. In the 1960s, in an interview, Richler had said that he felt closer to writers in New York or Chicago than, for instance, to those in Edmonton. The Jews' entitlement to Canada had also been problematic, due to an inherent anti-Semitism in the mainstream culture. The phrase "None is too many" is a blot on Canada's history, being an official's reply to the question of how many Jewish refugees could the country take during the war. Not surprisingly, for many Jews their perceived ideal homeland was Israel, and some of them left to settle there with its establishment in 1948. His own grandfather,

Jehudah Rosenberg, had bought property in Israel but died before he could emigrate, and Mordecai as a teenager had dreamed of becoming a pioneer in that land. Today these past attitudes might surprise some, but they also indicate what a long way the nation has come.

In the 1940s, Canada could still be considered a part and parcel of Britain's Empire. A decade later, however, as British power diminished, this dominion in the north was gradually emerging as an independent, influential nation on the world stage. From afar, in Europe, it is this newly assertive country in America that he would have perceived, in its entirety, as "home." During his return visits from Europe, he would now visit Toronto, which was gaining in importance and already was the nation's English-media capital, home to the CBC, the country's only national (English-language) newspaper, and the major publishers. He became increasingly better known as a novelist and commentator, with a distinct persona aided by his controversial, candid opinions. He travelled the country. Montreal, still, was his chosen place to live, when he ended his exile and returned for good; here he could go to Woody's or the bar at the Ritz to chew the fat over a Scotch, discuss the world; or take a walk down the old neighbourhood, stop for a smoked meat sandwich at Schwartz's, and never mind the fat. As he would say, "I could not live anywhere else in Canada but Montreal."

Soon after his return to Canada, Richler visited Yellowknife in the Northwest Territories. He enjoyed it immensely and took a charter flight north into the arctic barrens. He returned several times. Certainly there were problems there, particularly with alcoholism and unemployment. What he liked about it was its ruggedness, its honesty and lack of pretense, even as reflected in its terrain. It was cold and extreme, period. It came with its own sense of sardonic humour. It was not boring. No doubt he idealized it somewhat. And perhaps it reminded him of that essential quality of his father that he had come to love. He was charmed.

Following that first trip into the Arctic he began to conceive an ambitious novel that would embrace a Canada beyond Montreal's Jewish ghetto, over a longer historical and mythological span. Obviously he could not write about the WASPs or the French, the so-called founding nations; he would short-circuit them. It was, one would like to think, Richler's own embrace of his native country to which he had unequivocally committed. He read about the Franklin Expedition, the Arctic voyage in 1845 of the HMS *Erebus* and HMS *Terror* to discover a sea route from Europe to Asia, a subject that totally absorbed him. He researched, in addition, the myths of the Haida, a northwestern Aboriginal people, and life in nineteenth-century England. The book he produced was called *Solomon Gursky Was Here*. By his own confession, it was not easy to write. He finished it in 1989, more than a decade since he began to think about it. It is, technically, his most ambitious and riskiest book, linking his personally staked-out space of Jewish Montreal with the Canadian North, the rituals of Judaism with the rituals of the Inuit, the history of Canada with the history of the Jews. Daring and brilliant in its conception, it is in a sense a Jewish and personal appropriation of Canada.

Moving back and forth from the middle of the nineteenth century to the 1980s, telling the stories of numerous characters in many settings, the novel is held together by the obsession of Moses Berger, brilliant scholar and alcoholic, with the story of the elusive Solomon Gursky, one of three brothers, liquor barons who began in Yellowknife, the Northwest Territories, and amassed their fortune in the Prairies selling bootleg. But the Gurskys are no ordinary family from the shtetl. The first Gursky, Ephraim, the grandfather of the three brothers, is introduced to us with all his mythical potential as he descends from the sky, as it were—or from the North:

> One morning—during the record spell of
> 1851—a big menacing black bird, the likes of

which had never been seen before, soared over the crude mill town of Magog, hard by the Vermont border, swooping low again and again. Luther Hollis brought down the bird with his Springfield. Then the men saw a team of twelve yapping dogs emerging out of the wind and swirling snows of the frozen Lake Memphremagog. The dogs were pulling a long, heavily laden sled at the stern of which stood Ephraim Gursky, a small fierce hooded man cracking a whip.

Lake Memphremagog, in Quebec's Eastern Townships, incidentally, is also where Mordecai Richler had made his home, and where he finished this book. It is also where Moses, "Jeanne Mance born-and-bred" in Montreal's Jewish ghetto, now makes his home. As Moses goes about his quest, Solomon is presumed dead, and the Gursky empire, its headquarters in Montreal, is in the hands of his brother, the crotchety "Mr. Bernard." Moses is the son of L.B. Berger, a poet, who had accepted patronage from Mr. Bernard as his speech writer and cultural adviser. There is an obvious resemblance of the Gurskys to the Canadian liquor family of the Bronfmans, who had employed the poet A.M. Klein in a similar capacity to L.B.

The novel has the quality also of a mystery and reveals its secrets about the past (and present) in fits and starts. Ephraim Gursky, created by Moses from his researches, emerges as a trickster figure. A man of many abilities, he has worked as a coal miner, a thief, and a forger, and speaks English, Yiddish, Russian, and Hebrew. It turns out that he has an excellent singing voice too, and is in fact the son of a widowed Russian Jewish opera singer and cantor who ran away from a wicked stepmother. There is an element of the fairy tale, therefore, to his story. He easily acquires a knowledge of Latin, and though he may or may not observe a kosher diet, he knows his Scripture only too well. With him there is always his prayer shawl and silk top hat. While a convict awaiting deportation from London "to parts beyond the seas," he schemes by forging letters of recommendation to join the Franklin Expedition. Naturally he is virile, and fathers many children in various places. Ultimately he is the only man to survive the tragic expedition and sets his roots in Canada. Of his three grandsons, Bernard, Maurie, and Solomon, the latter is his favourite and becomes Moses Berger's obsession. It is Solomon who heard parts of Ephraim's story, which is revealed to Moses during his quest.

Solomon Gursky is considered by many to be Richler's best book, Canada's own example of magical realism. Moses's girlfriend reading Marquez's *One Hundred Years of Solitude*, the best-known founding text of magical realism, is surely Richler thumbing his nose at the critics: I know, I know. Whatever one calls it, the novel belongs to the class of works of the 1970s and 1980s that were involved with rewriting history—in the jargon, creating "subaltern history"—using both traditional and scholarly sources. Though the Arctic is emblematic of Canada, and is present in its mythic and geographic sense, it is the Jewish tradition that sings, loudly and richly. Yiddish expressions are scattered throughout, as are Biblical references. Ephraim Gursky, while surviving in the Arctic, bamboozles a group of Eskimos by "making" an eclipse come forth, and thus saves his skin. In the process he founds a Jewish sect, whose descendants wear parkas with four fringes hanging from them, each fringe made up of twelve silken strands; a kind of garment young Mordecai had to wear on St. Urbain as an Orthodox child, much to his discomfiture. It takes an advanced Sudoku-solver's resolve to follow Moses's pursuit of the clues that finally lead us to the mystery of Solomon Gursky, more elusive than his grandfather, a Scarlet Pimpernel and Jewish Avenger combined. Not quite the Horseman, but of the same ilk. We see him, or someone who looks like him, fleetingly, in Nairobi on the eve of the Israeli raid on Entebbe in the early 1970s; with

Marilyn Monroe in the 1960s; in D.C. during the Watergate crisis; running the Palestine blockade in 1948 using a freighter with the emblem of a raven.

That it had been a difficult book to write is acknowledged in the author's expression of gratitude to his wife, Florence: "Without her encouragement, not to mention crucial editorial suggestions, I would have given up on *Solomon Gursky Was Here* long ago."

WHEN *SOLOMON GURSKY* was published, Mordecai Richler was on the verge, sleeves rolled up, so to speak, of joining the battle for Canada, more precisely, Quebec. He was writing an article on the Quebec language crisis for *The New Yorker* and complained to an interviewer about how much he had to explain about Canada to American readers. But he was paid well. That article proved controversial, but the undaunted Richler followed it with a full-length book in 1992, *Oh Canada! Oh Quebec! Requiem for a Divided Country,* which became a national bestseller in a country anxious about whether it would survive intact. The book was not quite a requiem, however, though the situation might well have called for one in the near future; rather it was in part an explication of the crisis and in part a polemic to counter the claims and demands of the Quebec nationalists clamouring for greater protection of the French character and heritage of the province.

The issue of language rights had become the battleground for the nationalists, who claimed to fight for the French soul of Quebec, and the anglophones, who sought protection of their democratic freedoms. In 1977, the nationalist Parti Québécois under the charismatic premier René Lévesque passed Bill 101, the French Language Charter, which declared French the official language of the province and detailed a language policy. The charter went further than Bill 22 of 1974, the Official Language Act, under which French had already been declared the only official language of Quebec. Hitherto, under the British North America Act of 1867, the province had been officially bilingual. Bill 101 now explicitly made English and even bilingual commercial signs illegal. (Its other provisions put restrictions on children's education, and called for toponymic name changes.)

There were protests, the loudest in Montreal, which had long been a bilingual, commercial city, a metropolis of many cultures. Anglophones resorted to the national media for support and the courts for protection. Emotions ran high during this period, nationalist supporters of Bill 101 and "Francization" coming out in the streets in the tens of thousands. In 1988 the Canadian Supreme Court ruled that the sign provisions of Bill 101 were illegal in so far as requiring signs to be in French only. This did not end the matter; it was politics that ultimately reigned. Premier Bourrassa of Quebec promised to amend the bill and, using the "notwith-standing clause" to override the Canadian Charter of Rights and Freedoms, introduced Bill 178.

The arguments being made were those of intent, inter-pretation, and implementation: Should bilingual business signs be allowed, and if so, should they be allowed outside the business or only inside? What should be the permissible relative sizes of the texts in the two languages?

Reading about the conflict these many years later, one might well imagine oneself in the bizarre world of the Asterix comic books. What school boy or girl today would willingly knock their head against this dreary legal, political, provincial wrangle, find a jot of emotion in the issue? But this is where Richler weighed in, though he was led to remark,

> A Quebecker born and bred, I suffer from a recurring nightmare that all of us, French- and English-speaking, will one day be confronted by our grandchildren, wanting to know what our gen-eration was about when the Berlin Wall crumbled, a playwright became president of Czechoslovakia,

and, after seventy-four years, the Communist Party was overthrown in the Soviet Union.... We will be honor bound to reply, why, in Quebec, we were hammering each other over whether bilingual commercial signs could be posted outside as well as inside. We were in heat, not only in this province, but throughout Canada, over whether or not Quebec could be officially crowned "a distinct society."

The language conflict to him was a tribal quarrel that degraded both the English and the French speakers. But he was in it because Montreal was his city; he would point out the inconsistencies and pettiness of the nationalist arguments and at the same time highlight some relevant facts in Quebec's history.

A personal note is due here, from someone who had recently become a Canadian and had a stake in the outcome of the crisis. The issue was not only between the "English" and the "French."

From the vantage point of Toronto in the 1980s I couldn't help noticing in the nationalist rhetorics of Canada and Quebec a certain Third World, post-independence echo. This was evident in the prevalent insecurity vis-à-vis the United States, in the boosterism that was employed to counter it, and in Quebec's identity crisis. Among the top items on the list of any new African or Asian nation of the 1960s was, of course, the promotion of national culture, including the national language. But Canada was an older country. Hence the disappointing sense of déjà vu of a new Canadian upon arrival.

Ironically, and paradoxically, despite a mood of nationalist hostility against immigrants in Quebec and the fact that immigrants had not intended to come to a country threatening to break up, having already witnessed instability in their homelands, it was precisely because of having experienced liberation and nationalist struggles there that the situation of the French Québécois (as of the Aboriginals) could be viewed by them with a certain sympathy.

The French Québécois were a distinct people by their history, their language, and their culture. Their ancestors had been defeated and, an essentially rural people, they had lived under the British flag, dominated by an Anglo-Saxon political and business ruling class. This would be enough to garner them solidarity from much of the world. But it was a sleight of hand on the part of the nationalist demagogues to think of themselves as conquered natives. And isolationism is hardly the answer, when the rest of North America thrives upon the influx of new peoples, when even the European nations acknowledge their changing demographies. Richler, with remarkable perspicacity, notes that:

> As things stand now [1992], 40 percent of Canadians are of neither English nor French extraction. Surely within the next thirty, maybe even twenty years, they will form a majority of our population, and our children will not think it out of the ordinary to see Canadians of Chinese, Sikh, African, and Central American descent seated in Parliament alongside those of Polish, Greek, Ukrainian, and Italian origin already in place. Surely, too, these people will demand an end to the wasting tribal quarrel between the English and the French.

For many new Canadians, especially the educated ones, the prospect of another language for their children is in fact a thrilling one; knowing another language is a matter of distinction and pride. French traditionally has been the preferred second language, besides English, in many countries of origin. And, to complete the argument, if Quebec was a distinct society, French in Canada made the nation, too, a distinct one, gave it a certain oomph, a worldliness. It could not be mistaken for America. In Ontario, at least, French immersion programs have waiting lines for admission; parents harangue teachers to teach their children not just French grammar but to speak French; visitors to Quebec will nag their children to practise their French. And so for the French Québécois to turn against new Canadians was to poison genuine sympathy and produce dislike or at best indifference for Quebec. Meanwhile the immigrants kept coming into the rest of Canada, which celebrated its diversity and thrived upon it. Diversity and a positive attitude to change was *its* distinctness.

Richler's tone as he tackles the issue of Quebec is impatient, his polemic sharp. The extreme, ludicrous positions taken up by the language nationalists—for example, the vigilantes, or culture police, photographing English shop signs—and the exaggerated claims made by their polemicists—for example, comparing the plight of the French Québécois to that of the Eastern Europeans under Communism, or of the African Americans, who were enslaved, denied rights, and a minority in any case—are just the right targets for Richler's relentlessly quick pen. Ruthlessly he lampoons the idiocies, shows up the inconsistencies and fallacies of the ideologues, heaps scorn on the mendacity of the politicians. He points out at length how Quebec's nationalism is deeply rooted in its history of anti-

Semitism, which can be easily prompted to rear its head to this day; and he relishes in the reminder that the crowd that cheered de Gaulle's rallying cry "Vive le Québec libre!" delivered from the balcony of Montreal's Hotel de Ville would have included many of the supporters of Marshal Pétain during the Second World War.

As I watched the scene from Toronto, Quebec's language vigilantes could not but remind me of Tanzania's cultural vigilantes at the height of socialism in the early 1970s, who went around measuring the lengths of women's skirts and checked if a Coke bottle could pass through your pants, tight pants and short skirts having been deemed signs of Western depravity. On the other hand, the activists for English reminded me, through no fault of theirs, of a time when to converse in my native Cutchi in school was punishable. My own community of Indians in East Africa forewent their native tongue for English in schools, to great advantage, but then have always grappled for cultural integrity and memory. In Richler's own case, his ancestral Yiddish is a language arguably close to extinction. Language was an issue when I was growing up in Africa, and it has been an issue in modern India, as indeed in many other places. The case for French for Quebec, and indeed Canada, was not without support.

With its many digressions and its nonlinear exposition, Richler's book is not easy to read, except in parts where he entertains in his usual witty style. Moreover, not only the fact that it is written in English, but also the tone of voice suggests an English-Canadian and an American audience, with at times a certain anglo clubby smugness of the kind the English adopted toward their former colonies as the newly independent natives tripped themselves up in their nationalist zeal. Not surprisingly the Quebec intellectuals went apoplectic. His is a polemic, and he is not beyond taking the shortcut; he is also angry, frustrated, and combative; he will not avoid the barb, however irrelevant to his argument. And he has his favourite targets, everywhere in Canada. Why is it relevant that some of the Québécois are the descendants of prostitutes who were sent to the colony from France? (To be fair, he mentions also the dubious origins of the United Empire Loyalists.) What purpose is served by quoting himself, writing that Edmonton "is a city you come from not a place to visit ... a jumble of a used-building lot," with the character of "a boiler room"? And saying of the Maritimes, "wintering on welfare"? Surely he doesn't advocate the abandonment of such places? Is it fair to say of the *Canadian Forum* "well meant, but also as appetizing as health food. At worst, it publishes fiction and poetry that have obviously already been rejected by magazines that can afford to pay its contributors"? Surely he recalls his own penurious days as a beginning writer in Paris?

The pettiness of the "language wars," the threat of Quebec's secession, the mediocrity that he had an eye for, must have made him wonder at times if he had made the right decision after all in returning to Canada. He reveals a hint of his doubts, perhaps, when he states, "I am sometimes subject to fits of sentiment about this cockeyed country I grew up in and still call home." In frustration he says, "Sometimes it appears to me that Canada, even an intact Canada, is not so much a country as a continental suburb, where Little Leaguers govern ineffectually, desperate for American approval." What ticked him off this time was Prime Minister Brian Mulroney boasting to a *Time* reporter: "I am very good friends with George and Barb [Bush]." Alas, such cravenness in our politicians, when faced with the big boy, we have to put up with, as we put up with winter every year. As Richler had said, upon his return to Canada: "If we were indeed hemmed in by the boring, the inane, and the absurd, we foolishly blamed it all on Canada, failing to grasp that we would suffer from a surfeit of the boring, the inane, and the absurd wherever we eventually settled."

CHAPTER ELEVEN

True to Himself to the Last

Mordecai Richler's last novel, published in 1995, was *Barney's Version,* in which the protagonist Barney Panofsky, like the author, is a product of the Montreal ghetto and in his sixties. Crotchety in his older age, suffering from an enlarged prostate and progressive Alzheimer's, and acknowl-edged as having been something of a rogue, he is lamenting his desertion by his third wife and only true passion Miriam, who is now living with a featureless academic for whom he has only contempt. The novel is Barney's account of his life, his attempt to set the record straight, and is a somewhat meandering, though not incoherent, narrative reflecting his degenerating state of mind, partly defiant and angry, partly aggrieved. Like the author, Barney spent the years 1950 to 1952 in Paris, which is where he begins his story. There he had hung around with writers and artists, though not one himself, before starting a business and heading back to

Canada to become rich. Currently he is a producer of second-rate (as he readily admits) but lucrative television shows. Paris of the early 1950s plays a large role as a setting, but not the St. Urbain neighbourhood of the author's growing up, an essential feature of several previous novels. There are echoes from other Richler novels—Barney is a devoted family man (though the children are all adults now), having won Miriam after a relentless pursuit, and as the novel opens we learn that the shadow of a murder charge from the past hangs over him. However, this novel, narrated by the not quite reliable Barney, is different in tone from the previous ones and does not work over the same concerns. It is at its core the tender love story of an irrepressible but declining man, with a soupçon of mystery. We do not know if Barney's done it.

Richler had already shown signs of his own ailing while writing this work, having had a tumour removed in 1993; therefore there is in the novel a certain premonition of mortality. Remarkably, it may have been present as early as 1971, when in *St. Urbain's Horseman* Jake Hersh, at just about forty years of age, like Richler at that time, had worried about his failing body. In this final novel, Barney, like Mordecai, pays no heed to entreaties from family, eating what he wants to, drinking heavily, smoking cigars with abandon, not exercising. Richler's family could not make him give up his smoking and alcohol even during sickness. It was as if for him to hang on to life merely for the sake of breathing, giving up what was essential to it, was a copout. Just as taking the "lean" smoked meat option at Schwartz's deli, a definite no-no for aficionados, was dishonest. This was not how you ate a pastrami or a corned beef on rye. According to one anecdote, when a companion asked for the "lean" option at the deli, Richler told the waiter, "Put his fat on my plate."

In 1998 he underwent major surgery, in which one of his kidneys was removed. The recovery was painful and he had trouble breathing. Soon after, he began chemotherapy. News of his condition having spread, he was showered with honours and recognition. At the York University convocation in Toronto in May 1999, where he received an honorary doctorate, a paper cup of Macallan Scotch was placed obligingly on the podium for him. That year he also arranged a surprise birthday party for Florence, at the house of his friend Jack Rabinovitch in Toronto. Later, while on a lecture tour of Eastern Canada, he met his brother Avrum in St. John's, and when he said goodbye, he cried. In January 2001, Florence arranged a surprise birthday party for him in London, where his children and a few friends were present. In May 2001, he again went to Toronto, where he met his several friends. True to himself to the last, at a restaurant he had to drink his vodka and grapefruit juice with a straw. He had just returned from London, where his condition had deteriorated considerably. He died on July 3, in a Montreal hospital. He was seventy.

EVER SINCE HE LEFT Montreal for Europe, as a nineteen-year-old with no illusions but plenty of self-confidence and a demanding work ethic fuelled by an almost cocky ambition to be a great writer, Mordecai Richler's journey was one of constant self-discovery; his trajectory one of slow but ultimate return. He said he was not a Jewish or a Canadian writer, just a writer, echoing the claim of many a young writer refusing to be lassoed into a label. Both identities he found confining, belittling: one, though ancient and weighty, restricted him into an ethnicity; the other limited him to the corner of a small nation and its "picayune" concerns. His heroes, as a young man, were world writers; even when Canadian, they were of the world, though he knew of only one.

The distance to which he had escaped, the places where he chose to live—the great cultural capitals of Paris and London, an isolated fishing village off the coast of Spain—inevitably brought perspectives on home and belonging. His nostalgia was about Montreal, his stories were from that city. Montreal was his inspiration; it became his literary mission. Nourished on American culture and ambition, he was of a North American sensibility that set him apart from Europeans, but without doubt he was, specifically, a Canadian. In his columns, he wrote wittily and controversially about Canada, often out of frustration at the smallness of its national life, but always with concern. He wrote passionately about the Quebec crisis that culminated in the referendum of 1995. He wrote with equal passion against the mediocrity often lurking behind nationalism, draped, as he said, in the flag.

Reliving his life through his fiction, from childhood with its joys of youth and traumas of home, to middle age and past, he confronted his other inheritance, that of being a Jew and progeny of rabbis. Jewishness is a historical condition; how does one live it, when the rituals and practices are no longer meaningful? Unlike some of his American counterparts—comfortable as the bearers of their modern national identity—who have dealt with the issue in individualistic terms, Richler confronted it in mythic terms. His protagonists—Jake Hersh, Joshua Shapiro, and Solomon Gursky, in particular—take the historical burden upon themselves: images of the Inquisition, of the pogroms, of the Holocaust prey upon them even as they attempt to cope with their secular lives. Not surprising, perhaps, for an author strongly nurtured on the traditions. Not surprising, too, perhaps, for a Canadian for whom the national myth was too weak to compete. But always with that brand of humour that one might also call an inheritance, with which his fiction transcends sentimentality, earnestness, and rage.

There was a personal cost to his journey. His fiction at first alienated him from Jews, though later he came largely to be accepted by them; and, for reasons one only partly understands, there was a tragic break with his mother that was never reconciled. He became close to his father, who died when Mordecai was still in London, leaving him with the eternal regret of time not spent together. As Richler grew older, the qualities of honesty and working-class no-pretension that he saw as the hallmarks of his father were what he himself came to value most.

Richler's visit to Israel as he passed sixty enabled him to regard his dual inheritance once again, consisting of what he had described as the unequal burdens on his shoulders. It was a visit that turned him unusually reflective, his satirical scalpel put away for the most part; it made him reflect on his Orthodox childhood with some understanding and acknowledge his two grandfathers, one a rabbi, scholar, and writer and the other a shrewd businessman who had left behind his family in Galicia, Eastern Europe. Toward the end of his hyper-stimulative trip, he was finally led to confess:

> I was raised to proffer apologies because my ostensibly boring country was so short of history, but now, after five weeks in a land choked by the clinging vines of its past, a victim of its contrary mythologies, I considered the watery soup of my Canadian provenance a blessing. After traveling through the Rockies, Rupert Brooke had complained that he missed "the voices of the dead." Me, I was grateful at last for their absence.

Some years before, he had returned to Ibiza, the island off the coast of Spain, where he had spent some of his most creative and memorable months as a young man, completing a novel, but where he always thought he had left unfinished personal business behind. Realizing the obvious, that he had come chasing ghosts, he explained and understood his obsession this way: "It had to do with the good life I had made for myself. With Florence, with the children ... I appreciated that I had my family's love, and their respect, but I needed to feel entitled to it." He should not have run away from Ibiza, from the colonel, but it was over.

No better tribute could be paid by a man to his family. For someone whose childhood home had been unhappy, bitter, and humiliating, Richler had given himself a family that he valued perhaps above everything else. But there is a circularity here: his family gave him the emotional anchor that enabled him to write as fearlessly as he did.

What legacy did he leave behind? There are his numerous columns and articles, among which are important, thoughtful, and provocative contributions. He was always witty, at times hilariously so, and his satires held up a mirror to some of the absurdities of contemporary life, especially those pertaining to Canada. But perhaps he wrote too many, too quickly of these later in his life. They brought him an enthusiastic following even among those who would not read his fiction. How they will hold up in the future is any-body's guess. The numerous anecdotes told about him might well become part of a lasting legend. But it is his novels, in the pursuit of which he made the long journey out and back, that should ultimately count as his great legacy, and the con-flicted modern Canadian story that was his own life. Through the novels he broadened the cultural scope of Canadian fiction; he brought to it an exuberance it had not seen, with his vernacular, his wit, his indomitable though often tortured characters. Duddy Kravitz, Solomon Gursky, Jake Hersh, Joshua Shapiro, and Barney Panofsky—these will live on in the narrative and the imagining of Canada.

Books and Articles by Mordecai Richler

Richler, Mordecai. *The Acrobats,* 1954 rpt. (Toronto: McClelland & Stewart, 2002).

———. *Son of a Lesser Hero,* 1955 rpt. (Toronto: McClelland & Stewart, 2002).

———. *A Choice of Enemies,* 1957 rpt. (Toronto: McClelland & Stewart, 2002).

———. Conversation with Nathan Cohen. *Tamarack Review* 2, Winter 1957, p. 6.

———. *The Apprenticeship of Duddy Kravitz,* 1959 rpt. (Toronto: Penguin, 1959).

———.*Home Sweet Home,* 1960 rpt. (Toronto: Penguin, 1985).

———. "The White Americans," *The Spectator,* April 7, 1961.

———. "This Year in Jerusalem," *Maclean's,* August 11, August 25, and September 8, 1962.

———. *The Incomparable Atuk,* 1963 rpt. (Toronto: McClelland & Stewart, 1989).

———. *Cocksure* (Toronto: McClelland & Stewart, 1968).

———. *The Street,* 1969 rpt. (Toronto: Penguin, 2007).

———. *St Urbain's Horseman,* 1971 rpt. (Toronto: McClelland & Stewart, 2001).

———. *Shovelling Trouble* (Toronto: McClelland & Stewart, 1972).

———. *Notes on an Endangered Species* (New York: Knopf, 1974).

———. "Leaving School," *Illustrated Companion History of Sir George Williams University* (Montreal: Concordia University, 1977).

———. *Great Comic Book Heroes and Other Essays* (Toronto: McClelland & Stewart, 1978).

———. *Joshua Then and Now,* 1980 rpt. (Toronto: McClelland & Stewart, 1989).

———. *Solomon Gursky Was Here* (New York: Knopf, 1990).

———. *Broadsides* (Toronto: Viking, 1990).

———. *Oh Canada! Oh Quebec!* (Toronto: Penguin, 1992).

———. *This Year in Jerusalem* (Toronto: Knopf, 1994).

———. *Barney's Version* (Toronto: Knopf, 1995).

———. *Belling the Cat* (Toronto: Knopf, 1998).

———. "Return to Ibiza: A Memoir." Unpublished. Mordecai Richler Fonds, University of Calgary.

———. "The Rotten People." Unpublished. Mordecai Richler Fonds, University of Calgary.

Mordecai Richler Papers. Special Collections, University of Calgary Library.

William Weintraub Papers. For Richler-Weintraub, and Moore-Weintraub correspondence. Rare Books and Special Collections, McGill University Library, Montreal.

Concordia University (formerly Sir George Williams College) Archives, Montreal.

Other Sources

"A Pogrom in Galicia," *The New York Times*, April 21, 1918.

Anonymous. "Nite-Cap: a blemish on college due to closeness: one reporter's view," *The Georgia,* February 20, 1950, 13(17), p. 5.

Athill, Diana. *Stet* (London: Granta, 2000).

Bloom, Harold. ed. *Philip Roth* (Broomall, Pa.: Chelsea House, 2003).

Canadian Broadcasting Corporation. Available at: http://archives. cbc.ca/arts_entertainment/literature.

Craig, Patricia. *Brian Moore. A Biography* (London: Bloomsbury, 2002).

Gopnik, Adam, ed. *Mordecai Richler Was Here* (Toronto: Madison Press Books, 2006).

Kramer, Reinhold. *Mordecai Richler: Leaving St. Urbain* (Montreal and Kingston: McGill-Queens, 2008).

Lessing, Doris. *Walking in the Shade: Volume Two of My Autobiography* (London: HarperCollins, 1997).

Moore, Brian. "An Irishman in Malibu." Interview. Available at: www.laweekly.com/art+books/books/an-irishman-in-malibu/ 6888/?page=6.

National Film Board of Canada. *Ted Allan: Minstrel Boy of the Twentieth Century* (Montreal, 2002).

Posner, Michael. *The Last Honest Man: Mordecai Richler* (Toronto: McClelland & Stewart, 2004).

Rosenberg, Leah. *The Errand Runner* (Toronto: John Wiley, 1981).

Rosenthal, Herman, and S.M. Dubnow. "Hasidim, Hasidism." Available at: www.jewishencyclopedia.com.

Roth, Philip. *Goodbye, Columbus,* 1959 rpt. (New York: Vintage, 1997).

———. *The Counterlife* (New York: Vintage, 1986).

———. *The Facts. A Novelist's Autobiography* (New York: Farrar, Straus, & Giroux, 1988).

———. *Patrimony* (New York: Simon and Schuster, 1991).

Royal, Derek Parker. *Philip Roth: New Perspectives on an American Author* (Westport, Ct: Praeger, 2005).

Sampson, Denis. *The Chameleon Novelist: Brian Moore* (Toronto: Doubleday, 1998).

Schoenfeld, Joachim. *Shtetl Memoirs: Jewish Life in Galicia Under the Austro-Hungarian Empire and in the Reborn Poland 1898–1939* (Hoboken, New Jersey: Ktav Publishing, 1985).

Singer, Isaac Bashevis. *Satan in Goray,* 1955 rpt. (New York: Farrar, Straus, and Giroux, 1979).

Solecki, Sam. ed. *The Selected Letters of Jack McClelland* (Toronto: Key Porter, 1998).

Weintraub, William. *City Unique, Montreal Days and Nights in the 1940s and 50s.* (Toronto: McClelland & Stewart, 1996).

———. *Getting Started* (Toronto: McClelland & Stewart, 2001).

Wrobel, Pyotr. "The Jews of Galicia under Austrian-Polish Rule, 1867–1918." Available at: www.jewishgen.org/Galicia/html/Jews_of_Galicia.pdf.

ACKNOWLEDGMENTS

I am deeply grateful to Florence Richler for putting up with yet more interviews and queries, and for giving permission to quote material from the Richler Archives; and to Michael Levine for his generous assistance and clarifications throughout the writing of this book. I would also like to thank Jack Rabinovitch, Noah Richler, and David Staines for their reminiscences, John Ralston Saul for suggestions, Maya Mavjee for her interest, and Diane Turbide for her timely assistance. And finally, Nurjehan, for putting up with much endless chatter about M.R. and for reading the manuscript.

I would also like to express my appreciation to the University of Calgary Library, Archives and Special Collections; the Concordia University Archives; and the McGill University Library, Rare Books and Special Collections, for access and permissions; and especially to Appolonia Steele, Marlys Chevrefils, and Nancy Marrelli.

I have benefited greatly from two books on Richler, Reinhold Kramer's *Mordecai Richler: Leaving St. Urbain,* particularly for its exhaustive bibliography, and Michael Posner's *The Last Honest Man: Mordecai Richler,* for its extensive interviews. William Weintraub's *Getting Started:*

A Memoir of the 1950s is an invaluable, generous, and fascinating account of literary friendships involving an important chapter in the history of Canadian literature, and he deserves the thanks of all interested in the subject. Without his preserved letters and commentaries, much would have been lost.

1902 Moses (Moe) Richler is born in Poland.

1904 Shmaryahu Richler arrives in Montreal.

1905 Leah (Lily) Rosenberg is born in Poland.

1912 Jehudah Rosenberg arrives in Toronto.

1919 Jehudah Rosenberg arrives in Montreal.

1924 Lily Rosenthal and Moses Richler are married.

1931 Mordecai Richer is born on January 27 in Montreal.

1944 Lily and Moe's marriage is annulled.

1948 Mordecai Richler graduates from Baron Byng High School; he is admitted to Sir George Williams College.

1950 Richler departs for Europe in September.

1952 He returns to Montreal in September.

1953 Richler goes to London with Cathy Boudreau in August.

1954 His first novel, *The Acrobats*, is published in the spring. He and Cathy are married in August.

1958 Richler and Boudreau are separated in the summer.

1959   *The Apprenticeship of Duddy Kravitz* is published in the fall.

1960   Mordecai Richler and Florence Wood return to Canada in March and are married in Montreal in July.'

1961   The Richlers return to London in the spring.

1967   Moses Richler dies; Mordecai returns to Montreal for the funeral.

1972   The Richlers return permanently to Canada.

1974   Richler and his mother, Lily, stop speaking.

1992   Richler goes to Israel for the second time. He publishes *Oh Canada! Oh Quebec!* on the Quebec crisis.

1995   In the fall, Richler publishes his final and eleventh work of fiction, *Barney's Version,* which wins the Giller Prize.

1998   He undergoes major surgery.

2001   Mordecai Richler dies on July 3 in Montreal of cancer.